THE FORGOTTEN HERITAGE OF KILDARE

Jan '07

Happy Birthday John

Best Wishes.

Pat & Ella Fitzpatrick

THE FORGOTTEN
HERITAGE OF KILDARE

GER McCARTHY

NONSUCH

First published 2006

Nonsuch Publishing Limited
73 Lower Leeson Street
Dublin
Ireland
www.nonsuch-publishing.com

British Library Cataloguing in Publication Data.
A catalogue record for this book is available from the British Library.

ISBN: 1 84588 503 1
ISBN-13: 978 1 84588 503 8

Typesetting and origination by Tempus Publishing Limited
Printed in Great Britain

CONTENTS

FOREWORD

People of all ages, from Ireland and abroad, now have a chance to enjoy themselves by following in Ger McCarthy's footsteps. He has provided us with a handy guide to a county that is all too easily overlooked by those hurrying through Kildare to other destinations. Even people who live there, long-term residents or newcomers, are likely to learn something. McCarthy did not set out to say everything there is to be said about Kildare. His purpose is to highlight some aspects of its past that he believes are special.

Our built heritage is an intrinsic part of our history and communal identity. Therefore our attitude towards old buildings is an indicator of our attitude towards our society in general. We cannot and need not struggle to retain every house, castle and church indefinitely. Change is a healthy and natural process. But if we fail to treasure significant structures from the past, especially those that stand as special remnants of particular epochs, then we dishonour our ancestors and demean ourselves by neglecting our environment and forgetting where we came from.

Before we can appreciate our built heritage, we need to be able to find it. In the following pages, Ger McCarthy takes readers on a short trip through his beloved county. By following in his footsteps, we too may take pleasure in the beauty of places that he visits and learn more about those who went before us. McCarthy has written a guide that adults and children, citizens and tourists, can enjoy.

Ultimately, all history is local. As the author demonstrates, certain places are keys to an understanding of national history. There is a bonus for his readers in that, as well as introducing us to locations, he writes of some notable personalities who have lived in County Kildare.

The Curragh is perhaps the best-known location in County Kildare, thanks to the horse racing that takes place there (including Ireland's annual Grand National). The course at Punchestown is also a popular destination. McCarthy takes us beyond such landmarks to discover some of the other treasures of Kildare that lie down its many roads and lanes.

The author gives us glimpses of our social, cultural and political past that will prompt us to visit such locations for ourselves and help us to enjoy Ireland's built heritage as much as Ger McCarthy himself clearly does. In writing this guide to Kildare, McCarthy has done his home county a service.

Prof. Colum Kenny, Dublin City University

ACKNOWLEDGEMENTS

I would like to thank the following for their help with this publication: Brendan Cullen, James Durney, Larry Breen, P.J. Lydon, Dan O'Leary, Seamus Ahern, Tony Pierce and Karel Kiely. Mario Corrigan, Department of Local Studies in the County Library, Newbridge. Paula Doolin, archivist of the Loreto order central archives. Mr Jim Cannon, principal Gael-Choláiste Chill Dara. Liam Kenny for his photograph of Michael Lewis's name on the Menin Gate. To P.C. Behan and Brian McCabe a special word of thanks for their advice and help. Thanks to Elizabeth Trapp for the information on her uncle Fr Tom Murphy and for his photograph. Thanks also to Jacqueline Gavin née Price for her information on Ballyshannon House and Mary McNally for the information on Fr James Harold. To Betty Mullowney for the photograph of her late husband Lt. Col. Fintan Mullowney.

To Willie and Terry Giltrap who many years ago gave me a guided tour of Kilmorony and related the history of the Weldon family to me, and so started my interest in researching the history of the landed families of Kildare. Noelle Moran, formerly of Nonsuch Publishing, for her encouragement to publish this book. Thanks to Eoin Purcell and Kerstin Mierke of Nonsuch Publishing.

Thanks to the members of The County Kildare Federation of History Groups, and local historians from around the county who over the years attended my slide lectures on 'The Heritage and Houses of Kildare' and urged me to commit them to print. Special thanks to Joe Loonan for his technical support and advice with the transfer of my photographic slides to computer for this publication, and Sean Sourke for his excellent map of Kildare that will help readers to locate the sites mentioned in this publication. Thanks to Professor Colum Kenny for giving his time to reading my articles. To my wife Breda and family a special word of thanks for their help and support with this book.

BIBLIOGRAPHY

For further reading and more information on the monuments covered in this book, please refer to the following texts. The author has used these sources and found them to be very reliable.

Bence-Jones, M., *A Guide to Irish Country Houses* (Constable: London, 1988).

Burkes, *Peerage and Baronetage* (Burkes Peerage Ltd.: 105th edition, 1976).

Burkes, *Landed Gentry of Ireland* (Burkes Peerage Ltd.: 4th edition 1958).

Byrne, J., *Dictionary of Irish Local History* (Mercier Press: Cork, 2004).

Corrigan, M., *All that Delirium of the Brave–Kildare in 1798* (Kildare County Council: Naas 1998).

Costello, C., *Looking Back, Aspects of History Co. Kildare* (Leinster Leader Ltd.: Naas, 1988).

Cullen, S., *Fugitive Warfare 1798 in North Kildare* (CRS Publications: Clane, 1998).

Delaney, R., *The Grand Canal of Ireland*, (The Lilliput Press: Dublin, 1995).

Dooley, T., *The Decline of the Big House in Ireland* (Wolfhound Press: Dublin, 2001).

Dunlop, R., *Waters Under the Bridge* (Naas 1988).

Durney, J., *Far from the Short Grass* (Gall Press: Naas 1999).

Gilligan, B., *Teresa Brayton In an Irish Twilight* (The Teresa Brayton Heritage Group: Naas 2002).

Griffith, R., *Valuation of Tenements* (Dublin, 1850).

Harbison, P., *Coopers Ireland* (The O'Brien Press: Dublin, 2000).

Killanin, M.M., M. Duignan and P. Herbert, *The Shell Guide to Ireland* (Ebury Press: London, 1967).

Lawlor, B., *The Irish Round Tower* (The Collins Press: Cork, 1999).

Lewis, S., *A Topographical Dictionary of Ireland* (London, 1837).

O'Connor, E.A., *The Rebellion of James Eustace Viscount Baltinglass III* (MA Thesis, NUI Maynooth, 1989, unpublished).

Potterton, H., *Irish Art and Architecture* (Thames and Hudson: London, 1978).

Taaffe, F., *Eye on Athy's Past* (Ardreigh Press: Athy, 2000).

Tickell, F.E., *The Eustace Family and Their Lands in County Kildare* (J.K.A.S. Vol. XIII, Nos 6,7,8, 1955-1960).

Tillyard, S., *Citizen Lord* (Chatto & Windus: London, 1997).

Tillyard, S., *Aristocrats* (Weidenfeld & Nicolson: London, 1999).

Williams, J., *Architecture in Ireland 1837-1921*, (Irish Academic Press: Dublin, 1994).

Williams G.S., *The Racing Lodges of the Curragh* (Daletta Press: Kildare 1997).

Williams, J., *St. Mochua and The Round Tower* (South Dublin Libraries: Dublin, 2006).

Co. Kildare

Article Location Map

Map By Seán Sourke

A NOBLE COURT

Part of a wall is all that now remains of Harristown Castle, seat of the Eustace family from the fourteenth to the early eighteenth century. The following quotation from the *Complete Irish Traveller* gives some idea of what life was like at Harristown in the early eighteenth century:

Having visited Kildare, we set off for Kilcullen-bridge, and in our way thither, we visited the seat of Chetwode Eustace Esq., which is a fine large building, with a noble court before it, that bore the face of antiquity, but yet no decay appeared in any part. The situation is on the summit of a hill, and the front looks down from an high eminence into the River Liffey; but what charmed us beyond imagination was a vast body of water, in an artificial bed of a large extent, where we saw a ship completely furnished, as if ready to make a long voyage by sea; her sails spread, her colours flying, anchors weighed, guns firing, and the sailors neatly dressed, every one at their proper function, with their usual sea-terms. This gave us inexpressible delight.

In a neat pleasure-boat we were conveyed on board, where in a cabin finely adorned, we were seated, and served with an elegant entertainment by the worthy owner, and amongst the rest with sea provisions, biscuit, etc., the guns echoing round the adjacent woods and mountains, that seemed to us like a piece of enchantment; all this in a basin upon a high hill, I believe a hundred yards above a river, made by art, the bottom and sides paved. In short no description can reach it.

Though we were four hours in this agreeable employment, we were not cloyed; and when we came on shore, if we may call it so, we stood a long time on the delightful margin of the basin to admire the vessel, which was still under sail.

The gardens and groves are very large and extensive, the walls spacious, sheltered in several places with laurel hedges, finely kept, above twenty feet high, and two hundred yards in length; others with yew, and different sorts of holly, whose different greens give variety of pleasure. I must not forget to tell you that this artificial sea, as well as other variety of ponds, breed and feed innumerable carp and tench whose taste equals those of Hampton-court, the place most famed in England for those sorts of fish.

The seat is a corporation of itself, and sends two members to parliament, though there is no town on the estate, only the single house. The owner accommodates the electors with his hall, which is noble and spacious, and though he never covets to be one of the representatives, yet during the election, he generously treats all the voters, as well as the candidates.

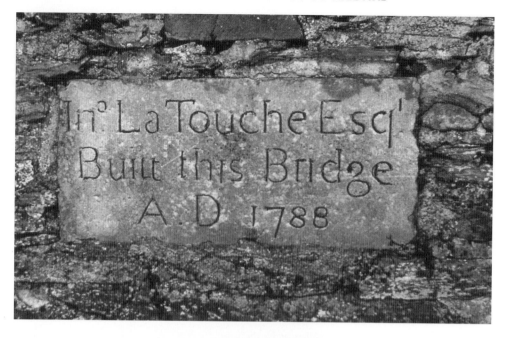

Above: A date stone from 1788 on Harristown Bridge.

Below: What remains of the wall of Harristown Castle.

ALEXANDER TAYLOR

Alexander Taylor (1746-1828), the renowned cartographer, was born in Scotland in 1746 and grew up in Aberdeenshire with his brothers George and William. Taylor started life as an estate surveyor in the Scottish Highlands. When the demand for estate surveyors declined he decided to join the army. He enlisted as a lieutenant in the 81st regiment of foot, otherwise known as the Aberdeen Highlanders, in December of 1771 and was soon on his way to Ireland. By 1776 Taylor was collaborating with Colonel Charles Vallancey in a military survey map of Ireland. Two years later, in 1778, he was working as a cartographer with his brother George and Andrew Skinner on *Taylor and Skinner's Road Map of Ireland*. In 1780 Alexander Taylor was assigned the task by the Kildare Grand Jury to survey and map the county of Kildare. The scale of the map is two inches to one Irish mile. His map was published in 1783, and was dedicated to Ireland's premier nobleman, the Duke of Leinster.

Alexander Taylor's headstone in Maudlins cemetery.

By the time the Ordinance Survey arrived in Ireland in the 1820s, Taylor's work had already been put to effective use. In 1788, his map formed one of the main sources for John Brownrigg's map of the Grand Canal. Later it was republished, reduced in size and with canals updated, in Rawson's *Statistical Survey of the County of Kildare.* Alexander Taylor married Elizabeth Bonner from Naas, and though he continued to hold property there, he settled more or less permanently in Dublin and occupied a fine house at Mespil Road near the Grand Canal. Taylor died in 1828 and was laid to rest in Maudlin's Cemetery, Naas, where a headstone records his name, age and army rank of Major. This early map of Kildare includes many features mentioned in this book, such as country houses, castles, churches, watermills, windmills, round towers and follies. The Taylor map is a good reference for all lovers of the heritage of Kildare.

ARTHUR WOLFE

Arthur Wolfe (1739-1803) was born on 19 January 1739 at Forenaughts House, Naas. He entered Trinity College Dublin in 1755, and graduated with a B.A. degree in 1760. At Trinity Arthur was dedicated to his studies, and having got his degree he continued to study for the bar, and entered the Middle Temple in London. At the age of twenty-seven, in 1766, he was called to the Irish Bar.

Forenaught House, the seat of the Wolfe family.

Although not a great speaker, 'for he was cold in manner and ungraceful in appearance,' his arguments were sound, his views were just, and his language so clear that he was greatly respected as an advocate. He quickly built up his legal practice into a successful business. Rising fast within the ranks of the legal profession, by 1787 he was Solicitor General and two years later he was Attorney General. In 1794 he was appointed Lord Chief Justice of Ireland.

Wolfe was also a member of the Irish House of Commons, having been provided with a seat in the House by Lord Tyrone. He represented the borough of Coleraine and later Jamestown in the Irish parliament.

Arthur Wolfe married Anne, daughter of William Ruxton of Ardee, Co. Louth. She was created a peeress in August of 1795 with the title Baroness Kilwarden of Kilteel, Co. Kildare. Arthur was made a peer after his elevation to the bench, and was given the title Baron Kilwarden of Newlands, Co Dublin. Two years later he was awarded the higher dignity of Viscount Kilwarden, and chose to be named Lord Kilwarden. In 1802 he was appointed Vice-Chancellor of Trinity College.

On the night of 23 July 1803, during the attempted rebellion led by Robert Emmet, Arthur Wolfe was killed while his daughter and his nephew Rev. Richard Straubenzie, rector of Kilbeggin Co. Westmeath, accompanied him in his carriage. As his carriage passed along James's Street into Thomas Street in Dublin, it was stopped and attacked by the rebels. One of the rebels asked who was in the carriage and Wolfe replied, 'It is I, Kilwarden, the Chief Justice'. A man said to be named Shannon came forward shouting 'Then you are the man I want', and piked him. His daughter remained in the carriage for a time, and it is said that Robert Emmet then took her to a nearby house. Wolfe's nephew, the clergyman, was also killed while trying to escape. Wolfe lived for a short time after the attack and was brought to the nearest watch-house. Before he died he overheard someone saying, 'The villains who committed such an act will be hung tomorrow'. Kilwarden was heard to say, 'Murder must be punished, but let no man suffer save by the just sentence of the law'. Lord Kilwarden was buried in the family vault at Oughterard near Kill, Co. Kildare.

ATHY MODEL SCHOOL

The Athy Model School was built in 1851 to the design of Frederick Darley (1778-1872), architect to the Commissioners of National Education. The building is of cut limestone with a high-pitched roof and tall chimneys built in the Tudor-Revival style. The model schools were established to facilitate the training of national school teachers.

Training took six months, during which time the candidate teacher lived and worked in a district model school. In 1840, the Commissioners of National Education proposed that the country should be divided into twenty-five districts with a model school located in a central position in each district.

The crane and water tower at Athy railway station.

The Athy Model School, built in 1851.

Athy Model School, which was designed by Frederick Darley.

Between 1848 and 1857, Darley built model schools at Athy, Ballymena, Belfast, Clonmel, Coleraine, Dunmanway, Galway, Kilkenny, Limerick, Newry, Trim and Waterford. Darley's department was phased out following a decision to transfer responsibility for national education buildings to the Board of Works.

Darley's last project for the Commissioners was the Central Model School in Gardiner Street Dublin, which later became a primary school. The Central Model School was to facilitate the further training of teachers who came from the country model schools. This building was destroyed by fire in 1982, and has been tastefully restored by the Department of Education.

Frederick Darley, a distinguished architect, was secretary of the Royal Institute of the Architects of Ireland. Among his other works were Merchants' Hall, and the library of the King's Inns, Dublin. He also designed a number of country houses including Coolbawn, a large Tudor-Revival house near Enniscorthy, Co. Wexford, which is now a ruin.

AYLMER MONUMENT, DONADEA

In St Peter's Church, Donadea, there is a splendid renaissance tomb – that of Sir Gerald Aylmer, who died in 1634. Undoubtedly the finest monument of its period in Co. Kildare, the monument has two niches containing the kneeling effigies of Sir Gerald and his second wife, Dame Julia Nugent, with their son and daughter.

The Aylmer and Nugent coat of arms are displayed and there are also interesting inscriptions on the frieze. Dame Julia Nugent was the daughter of Sir Christopher Nugent Lord Baron of Delvin, Co. Meath. Dame Julia died in 1617. The monument was originally in the nearby pre-Reformation church that is now a ruin. Sir Fenton Aylmer, seventh Baronet of Donadea, built St Peter's Church in the early nineteenth century, and had the monument re-erected in the new church in 1812.

The Aylmer name first appeared in Ireland towards the close of the thirteenth century. John Aylmer married Helen Tyrrell, daughter and heiress of John Tyrrell of Lyons, Co. Kildare. Through this marriage, the Manor of Lyons came into the possession of the Aylmer family. In 1588 Richard Aylmer of Lyons acquired from the Earl of Ormonde the entire Barony of Oughterany in north Kildare, which included the Manor of Donadea. His son, Gerald Aylmer of Donadea, was born in 1548, and became an eminent lawyer and a fearless advocate of religious tolerance who was imprisoned many times by Queen Elizabeth and James I. Sir Gerald was created first Baronet of Donadea, Co. Kildare, in 1622.

The Aylmer monument in St Peter's church, Donadea..

The Aylmer family remained in residence at Donadea for over three hundred years. The last member of the family to live in the castle was Caroline Aylmer, who died in 1935. Sir Richard Aylmer, sixteenth and present Baronet of Donadea, was born in Canada. He has made many visits to Ireland. In a lecture given to the Kildare Archaeological Society in St Peter's Church, Donadea in 1992, Sir Richard said that when the Aylmers make return visits to Donadea they feel they are among friends. The Land Commission acquired Donadea Castle and estate in 1936. The castle was dismantled and its contents auctioned. Donadea Demesne is now a forest park.

ST PAUL'S CHURCH BALLYSAX

Dedicated to St Paul, and built on the site of an earlier church, Ballysax church was built in 1826 on the instruction of Dr Lindsey, Bishop of Kildare. St Paul's was built to the design of John Semple in the Gothic style. Semple was architect to the Board of First Fruits, the body responsible for the provision of funds for the building of Church of Ireland churches, schools, and glebe houses. St Paul's rectory at Knocknagarm stood on nineteen acres and two roods. The cost of building the church was approximately £650, while the rectory cost just over £700. The Board of First Fruits had been set up in England to provide loans to the recently established Church of Ireland.

An additional feature of the building is the chancel, added around 1913, which housed a very beautiful ascension stained glass east window. It was donated by the Casey family in memory of Henrietta Laticia Casey, late of Newark House, Ballysax, and Raglan Road, Dublin. The stained glass window was removed and sold abroad in November 1984, against the wishes of the local community. They had sought to purchase the building and restore it for use as a heritage center for the community.

The building contains many wall plaques dedicated to former rectors and parishioners. There is also a baptismal font sculpted from a single block of granite, and a bust thought to be that of St Patrick, probably from the earlier church. On the south side of the church is a window donated by Germans who were interned on the Curragh during the Second World War. The graveyard contains the remains of many British soldiers who were stationed on the Curragh. Also in the churchyard is a good Doric obelisk monument to Robert Gore, founder of the Irish Turf Board.

An obelisk also marks the grave of the Rev. Dr George B. Wheeler (1805–1877), and the inscription 'He tried to do his best', sums up the life of this distinguished man. He was a lecturer in Classics at Trinity College, Dublin, and was the editor of *The Irish Times* from its foundation in 1859 until his death in 1877. He was ordained a minister in the Church of Ireland in 1865 and was appointed to Ballysax. The church was closed for public worship on 31 March 1974, when the parish became amalgamated with Newbridge Union of Parishes. The graveyard is an inter-denominational burial ground.

Ballysax church, designed by John Semple.

Ballyshannon House.

BALLYSHANNON HOUSE

The Annesley family built Ballyshannon House with material from the old FitzGerald Castle. The FitzGeralds had occupied Ballyshannon Castle from the close of the fifteenth century. A limestone slab with the initials MOH and the date 1620 was placed upside down in the wall on the southeast face of the house. On the side of the slab, a horse-like animal was carved into the stone. It probably came from the old castle, which was occupied in 1620 by James FitzGerald, who died in 1637. Over the hall door of the house a small human face in stone was built into the wall. It is said the stone came from a nearby inn, no longer in existence, called 'The Black Moor.' There is a townland nearby called Moortown. The moat at Ballyshannon is probably a pagan burial mound. The Annesley family was interred in a vault under the now disused Church of Ireland. This church is the successor of a pre-Reformation church on the site, and was dedicated to St James the Apostle.

Around 1800 Thomas Kennedy from Tipperary purchased Ballyshannon estate from the Annesley family. Thomas had six children: a son, Thomas, and five daughters. Thomas died young as a result of a riding accident. Only one of the five girls, named Mary Agnes, married. She married Edmund W. Murphy of Woodford House, Cashel, Co. Tipperary. They had a daughter, Barbara Murphy. Barbara married Thomas E. Price, eldest son of Richard and Charity Price of Ardmale House, Cashel, Co.

John and Mia Price with a photograph of Ballyshannon House in 1993.

Tipperary. They came to live in the Dower House at Martinstown on the Curragh – this house is now owned by Mr and Mrs Sage. Thomas and Barbara Price had two sons, Richard and Thomas William, and a daughter. In 1909 following the death of Ellen, the last of the five Kennedy sisters of Ballyshannon, her eldest grandnephew (Richard Price) inherited the estate. He died in 1915, and his brother Thomas took over the running of the estate.

Thomas William Price was by then married, with three sons. These three children are in the photograph taken on the front lawn of Ballyshannon House, with Thomas Richard (in the chair), Richard Francis, and John Edmund. The second photograph is of the adult John Edmund with his wife Mia, holding a framed photograph of Ballyshannon House, which they allowed the author of this book to copy.

The Land Commission took over the estate in 1959 and divided the land. The house was demolished and the timber from the roof was used in the restoration of Rothe House in Kilkenny. Sadly, the house and the date stone of 1620 have disappeared from the landscape of Kildare.

Barretstown Castle.

BARRETSTOWN CASTLE

Situated to the north of the town of Ballymore Eustace is Barretstown Castle. The core of the castle is an old Eustace tower house of the Pale. The Eustaces were one of the most distinguished of the names that came to Ireland at the time of the Anglo-Norman invasion. While not multiplying to the same extent as the Burkes, Butlers, FitzGeralds or other great Hiberno-Norman families, the Eustaces were numerous enough to be classed in Petty's 'census' of 1659 among the principal Irish names in four Baronies of Kildare.

The town of Ballymore Eustace was called after the Eustaces. In the fourteenth and fifteenth centuries they owned vast tracts of land in counties Kildare, Meath, Wicklow and Carlow. By the early years of the twentieth century the Eustaces and their descendants had disposed of most of their property and land in Co. Kildare. The last surviving relic of the Eustace family in Ballymore Eustace is the effigy of a Eustace knight, now preserved in St John's church.

Rev. Sir Erasmus Borrowes built the present Victorian Castle around the old Eustace tower house. Lt Walter Borrowes, Royal Navy, was born at Barretstown and was killed serving on a submarine on 23 January 1915. In St John's Church, Ballymore Eustace, a plaque records that he died in 'the German war.' The Borrowes continued to live at Barretstown Castle until 1919.

Sir George Murray, a Scotsman, then purchased the castle and estate. He converted the estate into a stud farm and planted many exotic trees in the grounds of the castle.

The Eustace effigy in St John's church, Ballymore Eustace.

Elizabeth Arden, the perfume manufacturer, bought the castle and estate in 1962. She commissioned the architect Michael Scott to carry out improvements to the interior of the castle. After Elizabeth Arden's death in 1967, Galen Weston bought the castle and estate; he carried out major works including the addition of a beautiful lake in front of the castle. The Weston family presented the castle and estate to the Irish Government in 1977, and for a period the government used the castle for meetings and conferences. Barretstown Castle and grounds are now a unique facility for sick children, set up in 1994 by the American actor Paul Newman.

Belan House, the seat of the Stratfords, Earls of Aldborough.

BELAN ORNAMENTAL TEMPLE

Travelers on the main Kilcullen-Carlow road at Bolton Hill will be aware of the Belan rotunda. This fine structure, built of Wicklow granite, is one of many follies, which included obelisks, in what was the parkland of the now demolished Belan house.

Belan House was built in 1743 for John Stratford, first Earl of Aldborough, to the design of the German architect Richard Castle, and the Irish architect Francis Bindon from Clooney, Co. Clare, and was one of the largest eighteenth-century gabled houses built in Ireland.

John Stratford, a member of parliament for the Borough of Dublin, enlarged and laid out the town of Baltinglass. After the rebellion of James Eustace, Viscount Baltinglass III, Baltinglass Abbey and lands were granted to the Stratfords. There is a fine pyramid mausoleum of the Stratfords at Baltinglass Abbey.

Edward Stratford, second Earl Aldborough, founded a cotton manufacturing industry in the village of Stratford-on-Slaney, Co. Wicklow, towards the end of the eighteenth century. He built a church and chapel in the village and encouraged settlers to come and work there. By the early nineteenth century up to one thousand people were employed in the mills, which were powered with water from the River Slaney.

It was Edward Stratford who built Aldborough House at Portland Row, Dublin. This house was completed on the eve of the 1798 Rebellion. He left a journal that gives a vivid and sad account of the 1798 Rebellion in South Kildare.

Belan Temple, one of the many follies in Belan demesne.

A benchmark on a doorway surround in Church Lane.

BENCH MARKS

On the limestone surround of a doorway at St David's Castle in the centre of old Naas, one will notice a benchmark that is 335.4 feet above sea level. Benchmarks were a system for height control used in the first Ordinance Survey mapping of Ireland. The first datum was the level of low water of spring tides observed at Poolbeg lighthouse in Dublin Bay on 8 April 1837, which was 8.22 feet below mean sea level. This datum plane was referenced to a benchmark on the base of Poolbeg lighthouse.

The Ordnance Survey was established in 1824, to provide a precise measurement of the townland, as a precursor to a nationwide valuation of buildings and land. They were based in Mountjoy House in the Phoenix Park in Dublin. Mountjoy House was originally built in 1728 as the country residence of Luke Gardiner. It later housed the mounted escort to the Lord Lieutenant who resided in the Vice Regal Lodge, now Áras an Uachtaráin. Mountjoy House and the surrounding buildings still serve as the headquarters of Ordnance Survey Ireland.

The original mapping of Ireland commenced in 1824, and Co. Kildare was mapped by 1839, with the rest of the country being completed in 1841. The majority of the maps were published in 1846. The printing plates for this map series were copper plates on which map details were all hand-engraved. As a result of the study of the tides in Ireland, mean

A mile stone with a benchmark on the Grand Canal near Digby Bridge.

sea level was also adopted as the datum by the ordinance Survey in England.

By 1958 there was growing evidence that a large number of benchmarks that formed a control network for height data had been destroyed, and it was considered necessary that a new leveling network should be established. At this time an automatic tidal gauge was set up at Portmore Pier, Malin Head, Co. Donegal. In 1972 the Ordnance Survey commenced the task of implementing all height data referenced to the Malin Head datum in all areas of new surveys.

With the huge urban and rural development that has taken place in Co. Kildare over the past ten years, a great number of benchmarks have been lost. Of the one hundred or so original benchmarks in Naas town only twenty-four have survived. Many fine examples can be seen on public buildings, churches, bridges gate piers and walls in other towns in the county such as Athy, Celbridge and Kildare town.

If you are removing an old building, stonewall or gate pier, keep an eye out for the old 'Crow's Foot' and don't dump it with the rubble.

Bert House, which was built for William Burgh.

BERT HOUSE

Bert House was built between 1725 and 1730 for William Burgh, who was Comptroller and Accountant General for Ireland. He was born in Dromkeen, Co. Limerick in 1667, son of Right Rev. Ulysses Burgh Bishop Ardagh. Bert House is attributed to William's brother Thomas Burgh (1670-1730), who was Engineer and Surveyor-General for Ireland. He settled in Naas and in 1709 built Oldtown House to his own design. His descendants still reside at Oldtown. Other buildings attributed to Thomas Burgh include Oakley Park House and the Charter School in Celbridge. He also designed the library of Trinity College, Dr Steeven's Hospital, and the Royal Barracks (now Collin's Barracks) in Dublin.

William Burgh's only son, Thomas, was born in 1696 and succeeded him at Bert ouse. William's daughter Elizabeth married Anthony Foster in 1734. Their son John was the last Speaker of the Irish House of Commons. Thomas Burgh sat in parliament as the member for Lanesborough, Co. Longford. He was a freeman of Athy Borough and served as Sovereign of Athy in 1755. He married Anne in 1731. She was the daughter of Right Rev. Dive Downes, the Bishop of Cork and Ross, whose wife Catherine was a sister of Robert, the nineteenth Earl of Kildare. Ann's brother, Robert Downes, was later to sit as MP for Kildare and he was Sovereign of Athy in 1749.

Thomas Burgh died in 1758 and was succeeded by his eldest son, William, who was born in 1741. William was the first Burgh of Bert House to represent Athy in parliament, which he did between 1768 and 1776. He was associated politically with Horace Walpole and he died in York in 1808. A monument to his memory, by the English neoclassical sculptor Sir Richard Westmacott (1775-1856), is to be found in York Minister Cathedral.

William left no heir and his younger brother Thomas succeeded him in Bert House estate in 1808. He was the MP for Athy until 1790. Thomas' daughter Ann maintained the parliamentary connection when she married in 1767. She married her second cousin, Walter Hussey Burgh, who was born at Donore House, Caragh Co. Kildare. He distinguished himself as one of the most eloquent advocates at the Irish Bar and the finest orator of his day. He represented Athy Borough Council in the Irish House of Commons between 1769 and 1776.

On the death of Thomas Burgh in 1810, Bert House passed to his only son, Ulysses. Born in 1788, Ulysses married Maria Bagenal of Bagenalstown Co. Carlow in 1815. He was a member of the Borough Council of Athy until its disbandment in 1840, and served as Sovereign of Athy in 1834, and again in 1840. The last Town Sovereign of Athy was Rev. F.S. Trench of Kilmorony House.

Ulysses Burgh succeeded to the title of second Lord Downes in 1826 on the death of his cousin William, first Lord Downes, who was appointed Lord Chief Justice following the assassination of Lord Kilwarden during the Robert Emmet rebellion. William Downes, son of the former Sovereign of Athy, Robert Downes, had been created first Lord Downes in 1822, on his retirement as Chief Justice. Having died without male issue, the title passed to his cousin Ulysses Burgh of Bert. It was Ulysses Burgh, by then second Lord Downes, who presented the Town Hall clock to the people of Athy in 1846.

When Lord Downes of Bert died in 1863, his eldest daughter Charlotte, who had married Lt. General James Colborne in 1851, succeeded him. He was the son of John Colborne, who led the decisive movement of the 52nd Light Infantry, which secured the victory of Waterloo. He was later Commander-in-Charge of the British Army in Ireland and was raised to the title of Lord Seaton in 1839. Charlotte's husband, James Colborne, succeeded to her father's title in 1863, and it was as Lord and Lady Seaton that James and Charlotte came to live in Bert House following the death of Lord Downes. Bert House remained in their ownership until 1909, when it was sold to the Geoghegan family. The Burgh, Downes, and Geoghegan families are interred in Kilberry churchyard. Bert House is now a hotel.

BORROWES OF GILLTOWN

Entrance gates with piers surmounted by lions mark the entrance to Gilltown estate. Gilltown is one of the finest remaining walled estates in Co. Kildare, and was the home of the Borrowes family for three centuries.

The Borrowes name first arrived in Co. Kildare towards the end of the sixteenth century. It is recorded that, at the outbreak of rebellion in Ireland in 1641, Erasmus Borrowes deposed that he was unable to resist the Irish, and that he had lost in goods, corn, and cattle at his several houses of Grangemellan, Gilltown and Carbally £9,396; in debts £11,932 and a yearly income of £1,200 or thereabouts. 'For his many good and faithful services to the kingdom, both in war and peace', he was created a Baronet

Gilltown House, the eighteenth-century seat of the Borrowes.

of Ireland by King Charles I in July 1645. Like many of their class, the Borrowes married into families of wealth and influence. Sir Walter Borrowes, second Baronet of Gilltown, married Lady Eleanor FitzGerald, daughter of George, sixteenth Earl of Kildare, the ceremony being performed with great pomp before the Lord Mayor of Dublin in February 1656.

As with many of the landed gentry, the Borrowes gave service to church and army. Reverend Erasmus Dixon Borrowes was rector of Ballyroan, Co. Laois. On the death of his brother he became the eighth Baronet of Gilltown. Sir Erasmus Dixon Borrowes, ninth Baronet, served in the Burmese war of 1853 and in India, where he was wounded. His son Walter served in the Royal Navy in the First World War and was killed in action in January 1915. There is a plaque in St John's Church, Ballymore Eustace, commemorating his death in 'the German War'. Sir Erasmus Dixon Borrowes was succeeded by his eldest son, Sir Kildare Henry Borrowes, tenth Baronet of Gilltown, who was a Justice of the Peace and Deputy Lieutenant for County Kildare and, from 1902, High Sheriff of the county. He was for a time A.D.C. to the Lord Lieutenant of Ireland. He served as a draft-conducting officer in the First World War.

Sir Kildare Henry Borrowes died without issue in 1924, and was succeeded by his brother Sir Eustace Dixon Borrowes, eleventh Baronet. He was the last of the family to live at Gilltown. His only son, Kildare Henry, like his uncle Walter, served in the Royal Navy, and was killed while serving on board the *HMS Queen Mary* at the Battle of Jutland in May 1916. The Borrowes of Gilltown, like many other landed families, never recovered from the loss of life suffered in the Great War. Hubert Edward Madden Bourke assumed the additional surname of Borrowes on inheriting the Gilltown estates. He sold the estates in 1925, ending the Borrowes connection with Kildare after three hundred years. Many generations of the Borrowes are buried in a pyramid mausoleum near the old church ruin in Gilltown estate.

The Borrowes coat of arms.

Above: The entrance gates to Gilltown Estate.

Right: The Borrowes mausoleum on the Gilltown Estate.

Carbury Castle, built on the site of a medieval castle of the Berminghams.

CARBURY CASTLE

On the hill of Carbury in North Kildare are the much-neglected ruins of Carbury Castle, a fortified Jacobean manor house with tall chimneys. The first proprietor of the area was the Anglo-Norman Meiler Fitz Henry who was granted the district by Strongbow. The Birminghams acquired the castle and surrounding district in the fourteenth century, and were to become the most dominant family in the area for centuries.

In 1542, Henry VIII granted to Sir William Bermingham the title of Baron of Carbury, as well as the site of the priory of Ballyboggan, and the Abbey of Clonard. The Irish Deputy, who had summoned him to parliament in Dublin the previous year, had already conferred the title 'Baron of Carbury' on him.

Sir William went to that parliament as Baron of Carbury and assisted, with the other magnates, at solemn High Mass on Corpus Christi day. He rode in the procession to the parliament house, and voted with the others for the abolition of the Papal jurisdiction within these realms, and for the transfer of that jurisdiction to King Henry VIII.

It was said that there was great rejoicing in Dublin on that occasion. Bonfires were lit throughout the city, and wine was freely distributed to the people. The king granted a general amnesty, and freedom to all persons confined in jail. The Baron of Carbury was married firstly to Rose, daughter of Gerald FitzGerald of Blackwood Castle, and later to Anne, daughter of Sir John Plunkett of Beaulieu, Drogheda, Co. Louth.

Chimney detail at Carbury Castle.

The ruins of Dunfirth church.

An effigy of Sir William Bermingham, in the Dunfirth church ruins.

Sir William died in 1548 and was buried at Dunfierth, near Johnstown Bridge. His effigy and the side panels from the altar tomb are preserved in the mortuary chapel of the now ruined church. Sir William is depicted in armour with his head on a cushion, which has shields bearing the arms of the Berminghams, and Sir William's two wives. His feet rest on a lion. He wears a crucifix on his chest, and holds a sword with both hands.

Queen Elizabeth granted Carbury Castle to Sir Henry Colley in 1562. Through marriage the castle came into the possession of the Wellesleys, ancestors of the 'Iron Duke' of Wellington.

The Castledermot Round Tower and Romanesque doorway.

CASTLEDERMOT ROUND TOWER

The Monastery on this site began life as Disert Diarmada, a hermitage founded in 812 by St Diarmaid. The Vikings plundered the monastery twice in the ninth century, and it was burned in 1106. The only parts of the monastery that survive are a tenth-century Round Tower, two ninth century High Crosses, and the reconstructed Romanesque west door of an earlier church. The Round Tower is unusual first of all in having its entrance only slightly raised above ground level, and secondly in being to the north of the church (Round Towers are normally to the west of churches).

The tower is twenty metres high and is built of random rubble granite stones. St James' Church of Ireland was connected to the tower when it was built in the early nineteenth century. The upper portion of the tower is a reconstruction dating from the early eighteenth century, and may have been built at the same time that the bell in the tower was installed – when the tower was adapted as a belfry to the church. The bell, dated 1735, still hangs in the bell-floor of the tower.

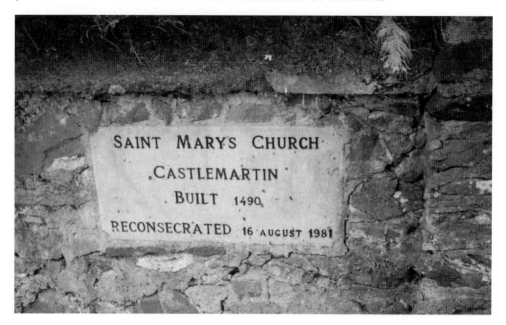

A date stone on St Mary's Church, Castlemartin.

CASTLEMARTIN HOUSE

Castlemartin is an early eighteenth-century house built around 1720 on the site of a Fitz Eustace Castle. The first Fitz Eustaces arrived in Ireland at the time of the Anglo-Norman invasion, and by 1317 they had established their chief residence in Kildare at Castlemartin. The last of the Castlemartin Fitz Eustaces left Ireland with the Wild Geese.

Sir Thomas Keightley, MP for Co. Kildare, acquired Castlemartin in the early eighteenth century. He died in 1718 without a male heir. A wealthy Dublin banker named Harrison then purchased the estate, and it was he who built the present house. Harrison appears to have lived at Castlemartin for only a short period, as the house was sold to the Right Honorable Thomas Carter around 1730. He was Master of the Rolls in 1731, and Secretary of State in 1755. During the rebellion of 1798, Lt General Sir Ralph Dundas used Castlemartin as his headquarters. Dundas took the surrender of the rebels on Knockaulin Hill after the battle of Old Kilcullen. It was from Castlemartin that he issued his proclamation that led to the massacre at Gibbeth Rath on the Curragh on 31 May 1798.

Thomas Samuel Blacker purchased Castlemartin house and estate in 1854. The house faces along a straight avenue of lime trees at the end of which are magnificent eighteenth-century wrought iron entrance gates. On the death of Mrs Blacker in 1967, the house and estate were inherited by her grandnephew Lord Gowrie, the politician. Dr Tony O'Reilly purchased Castlemartin House and estate, and has restored the house to its former splendor.

Castlemartin House, which is now owned by Sir Anthony O'Reilly.

St Mary's church, Castlemartin, when it was in ruins.

St Mary's Church, Castlemartin, after it was restored.

The entrance to the ice house in Castlemartin.

In the grounds of Castlemartin beside the River Liffey there is a medieval manorial church built in 1490 and dedicated to St Mary. Inside the church is an altar tomb of a Eustace knight. His effigy lies on top of the altar tomb, the side panels of the tomb have various biblical and ecclesiastical figures carved on them, and one panel bears the Eustace coat of arms. The ruined manorial church of St Mary's has been restored, and the altar tomb reassembled under the guidance of the renowned architect Percy La Clerc. St Mary's church was re-consecrated in August 1981.

CELBRIDGE ABBEY

Celbridge Abbey was built by Bartholomew Van Homrigh, a wealthy Dutch merchant who was Lord Mayor of Dublin in 1697. He secured from William of Orange the chain of office that is still worn by the Lord Mayor of Dublin. Esther Van Homrigh, his eldest daughter, was the beloved 'Vanessa' of Jonathan Swift, who was Dean of St Patrick's Cathedral in Dublin from 1713 until his death in 1745. Swift, renowned for his satire *Gulliver's Travels*, frequently visited Vanessa at Celbridge Abbey. Vanessa cherished these visits, and was obsessed with him to the point of planting a laurel in the grounds of the abbey to commemorate each visit. The relationship, stormy and enigmatic, continued for some years, until Vanessa heard rumours about her rival Stella Johnston, whom Swift is believed to have married. Vanessa never recovered from the shock and died of a broken heart at the age of thirty-four, in 1723.

Celbridge Abbey, once the home of Ester Van Homrigh – 'Swift's Vanessa'.

Chief Justice Thomas Marlay, whose daughter married James Grattan, father of the statesman, orator, and patriot Henry Grattan, then purchased Celbridge Abbey. It was Henry Grattan who rebuilt Celbridge Abbey in its present Georgian-Gothic style, towards the end of the eighteenth century. Grattan loved the abbey and grounds, which are said to have inspired his patriotism. Speaking of his dedication to fighting for an independent parliament for Ireland he said; 'Along the banks of the Liffey amid the groves and bowers of Swift and Vanessa, I grew convinced that I was right. Arguments unanswerable came to my mind, and what I then presaged confirmed me in my determination to persevere.'

Beautifully situated on the banks of the River Liffey, the grounds of Celbridge Abbey have been developed into theme walks. Life-sized figures portray the relationship between Swift and Vanessa, and Grattan's fight for Irish nationalism. In the grounds are 'Vanessa's Bower' and the Rock Bridge, believed to be the oldest footbridge across the Liffey.

The St John of God Brothers acquired Celbridge Abbey and grounds in 1957, to serve as a community house to the nearby St Raphael's, a residential school for the disabled.

CELBRIDGE CHARTER SCHOOL

Celbridge Charter School or Collegiate College was built with funds provided by the Conollys of Castletown House. William Conolly, Speaker of the Irish House of Commons, rose from a modest beginning to become the richest man in the Ireland of the day. His house at Castletown was the largest of the great Irish houses built in the Palladian style.

William Conolly died in 1729, and in his will he bequeathed money to have the Charter School built. His widow Katherine had the school opened in 1732. In the early years the school accommodated forty girls who were to be 'lodged, clothed and dieted' there. The aim of the school was to rescue the children of the 'poor natives' from ignorance, and superstition and to instruct them in the English tongue, manners, and Protestant faith.

The school was built on fifty acres of land on which flax was grown, and the students were employed in the cultivation and harvest of the crop, right through to the manufacture of linen. In the early nineteenth century, over one hundred students were in the school.

There were Charter Schools at Celbridge, Carbury, Maynooth, Castledermot and at Monasterevin. The latter is now in a poor state of repair, and is known locally as the 'Hulk'. The Charter School at Carbury was sacked and burned during the 1798 rebellion.

The Celbridge Charter School was designed by the architect Thomas Burgh MP, Engineer and Surveyor-General of Ireland, and is a fine early Georgian building with an imposing triple pedimented entrance gate. In later years the school became a Collegiate Boarding College, which closed in 1972. The building is now a hotel, and its eighteenth-century character has been charmingly retained by the owners.

Celbridge Charter School, which is now a hotel.

CHURCH OF OUR LADY AND THE GUARDIAN ANGELS

Before the First World War the people of Sallins requested of their parish priest, Father Norris, that a chapel be built in Sallins village in the parish of Naas, to save parishioners the journey to Naas for Sunday Mass. A committee was formed and raised a total of £400 before the outbreak of the war.

Father Norris, then parish priest of Naas (he lived to be one hundred and three years old) had intended to build a new school for Sallins, and to convert the old school into a chapel. He had bought the site for the school before the war broke out. The project was put on hold during the war years and during the troubled years leading up to the foundation of the Free State. As building costs soared and building grants dried up, plans for a new school were shelved. In 1923, it was decided to construct a church at a low cost on the site that Father Norris had initially bought for the planned school.

The contract for the building was given to Messrs Harrison & Co. of Camberwell, London; the building was completed in 1924. The firm brought over some of their own staff from England, and one of them, Edward Laxton, settled in Sallins. Local tradesmen contributed to the construction, and the seats were a gift from Father Norris and were made by Corcoran brothers of Naas. The interior timberwork was by Smyths of Sallins. The stained glass window by Meyer of Munich was a gift from

The church of Our Lady and the Guardian Angels, Sallins.

the Bushell family of Naas. From 1800 the Bushell family carried on a very successful shoemaking business in the town. Their premises on Main Street were burnt in 1922 during the Troubles and later rebuilt. The business continued into the early 1960s and the premises are now part of the *Leinster Leader*.

Father Norris PP dedicated the church on Sunday 5 October 1924. The bishop, Dr Foley, was unable to travel up from Carlow to perform the ceremony, as he was unwell. At the dedication Father Norris said the church had been built free of debt at a cost of £870. Sallins Church was a chapel of ease in Naas parish. Bishop Patrick Lennon constituted Sallins a new parish in 1973. Father Laurence Newman who had been a curate in Naas in the 1950s was appointed the first resident parish priest of Sallins.

CLONGOWES WOOD COLLEGE

Clongowes Wood College, formerly known as Castle Browne, is a much-altered Eustace Castle, which was a border fort of the English Pale. The outline of the Pale is still visible near the college. The castle and lands were forfeited because of the Eustace participation in the Catholic Confederation.

The Brownes purchased the castle and estate in 1667, and intermarried with the Wogan family from nearby Rathcoffey Castle. Clongowes Wood was re-built in the

Clongowes Wood College, now a Jesuit boarding school.

The 1929 block , which was designed by Tom Cullen.

Gothic Revival style in 1788, by Thomas Wogan Browne, who acted as his own architect. He added corner round towers and Irish battlements to the castle. General Michael Wogan Browne was A.D.C. to the King of Saxony. Wogan Browne was a distinguished soldier and marched to Russia with Napoleon, and later represented the King of Saxony at the congress of Vienna in 1815.

Wogan Browne sold the castle and estate to the Society of Jesus, who opened a school for boys there in 1814. Samuel Lewis in his *Topographical Directory of Ireland* (1837) refers to Clongowes Wood as 'A College for the education of the Catholic nobility and gentry'. Many distinguished people attended the school, including Thomas Francis Meagher, 1833-1839; John Redmond, 1868-1874; and James Joyce, the author of *Ulysses*, who came to Clongowes in the autumn of 1888. When he arrived at the school he was only six and a half years old, and his nickname there was 'half-past-six'. Joyce spent three and a half years in Clongowes, and left at Christmas 1891.

The Boys' Chapel was built in 1907 to the design of Ashlin and Coleman architects. The chapel has Stations of the Cross by Sean Keating (1889-1977), and a series of beautiful stained glass windows by Michael Healy (1873-1941) and Evie Hone (1894-1955).

Construction work started on the 'new building' in 1929 and was completed in 1932 to the design of Tom Cullen, who had attended Clongowes as a student (1896-1897). The contractor was T.R. Macken of Dublin. The building was intended to modernize and enlarge the school's facilities in order to provide for 325 boys and ensure that the school could 'bear comparison with the great and historic schools of any country in Europe'.

The Conolly Obelisk, often referred to as Conolly's folly.

CONOLLY OBELISK

Often referred to as 'Conolly's Folly,' the obelisk at Castletown was built in 1740 by Speaker Conolly's widow, Catherine, and has been attributed to the German architect Richard Castle. At the time, Castle was working on the remodeling of Carton House for Robert FitzGerald, nineteenth Earl of Kildare. The obelisk, forty-four metres high, closes the vista at the back of Castletown House. The obelisk was built to provide work for the poor of Celbridge and the surrounding area after the severe winter of 1739.

The FitzGeralds and Conollys were later connected through the marriages of Louisa and Emily Lennox, daughters of the second Duke of Richmond. Louisa married Thomas Conolly of Castletown. Emily married James FitzGerald, first Duke of Leinster, and was the mother of Lord Edward FitzGerald, military commander of the United Irish Forces during the 1798 rebellion.

COUGHLANSTOWN CROSS SHAFT

In the townland of Coughlanstown is the ruin of a medieval church dedicated to St James. Located inside the church ruin is the limestone shaft of a memorial cross of the Eustaces. The inscription on the front of the shaft reads 'Eustace Lord Portlester 1462.' Roland Eustace was son of Sir Edward Eustace of Castlemartin. Along with Harristown they were the principal seats of the Eustaces from the fourteenth century onwards. Lord Portlester died in 1496 and is buried at New Abbey Kilcullen, where there is a fine double effigy of him and his wife Margaret D'Artois.

The date 1462, on the cross-shaft at Coughlanstown, is the year Roland Eustace was elevated to the title Baron Portlester. He was one of the first Irish peers to be so created by Letters Patent. The only other Irish peerages granted before the year 1500 were those of the Earls of Ulster, Carrick, Kildare, Louth, Ormonde, Desmond and Waterford; Viscount Gormanston 1478, and Barons Trimbleston 1462, Portlester 1462, and Ratowth 1468.

The Eustace coat of arms is carved on the reverse side of the cross-shaft. The crest of the town of Naas, represented by a vertical snake, is cut on one side of the shaft. The other surviving early example of the crest of Naas, a coiled snake, is to be found on the foot of the Mace of Naas, now in the National Museum of Ireland.

The cross shaft in the ruins of St James' Church, Coughlanstown.

A roadside cross in Coughlanstown.

Jim and Ann Maher beside the Bonham coat of arms at Crookstown Mill.

CROOKSTOWN MILL

At Crookstown, beside the Quaker village of Ballytore, is the last working corn mill on the River Griese. Along the length of the river are the ruins of many old water mills. The River Griese rises at Tober near the town of Dunlavin, Co. Wicklow, and flows through south Kildare, and enters the River Barrow in the townland of Jerusalem south of Athy.

John Bonham built Crookstown Mill in 1840. His family seat was at Ballintaggart, Colbinstown. The Bonhams had settled at Ballintaggart in the early eighteenth century and continued to live there until the property was sold in 1931. The Bonham family had a long tradition of service in the British army, from the Crimean War to the Second World War.

The late Mr Jim Maher and his wife Ann purchased Crookstown Mill in the early 1970s. The mill had fallen into ruin, and it took many years of hard work by Jim and his family to restore it to a working mill. All the old features of the mill have been preserved, including the breast-shot water wheel. The interior workings of the mill as well as the set of three millstones have been maintained in running order. A ship's wheel, salvaged from a ship belonging to the Bonhams, operates the sluice gate of the mill. At the entrance to the mill there is a sculptured limestone plaque with the Bonham family crest and motto.

CURRAGH GRANGE

Curragh Grange House on the edge of the Curragh was built for Henry Greer in 1904 to the design of Richard Orpen. The house, in the Queen Anne style, is built of red brick with pebbledash. In July 1912 Henry Greer and his wife hosted a fête at Curragh Grange in aid of the Drogheda Memorial Hospital on the Curragh. The Greers were guests at the official opening of the hospital in April 1899. Lady Aberdeen, wife of the Lord Lieutenant, motored down from the Vice Regal Lodge for the occasion.

In the early years of the twentieth century Henry Greer set up Tully Stud in Kildare town for Colonel William Hall Walker, later Lord Wavertree. The colonel had purchased the land from James Fay, a local farmer, in 1900. Under the management of Henry Greer, Tully became one of the best stud farms in Europe at that time. Colonel Hall Walker decided to have a Japanese garden built on boggy land near Tully House. He employed the eminent Japanese landscape gardener Tassa Eida to lay out the gardens with the help of a large number of local labourers.

Curragh Grange House, which was built for Henry Greer.

The British government purchased Tully Stud from Colonel Hall Walker in 1916 and set up the National Stud there, with Henry Greer becoming its first director. In 1943 the Irish government took over the land and buildings at an agreed valuation from the British Government. The Irish National Stud Company was formed in 1945, and officially took over the National Stud on 31 August 1946. The National Stud and Japanese Gardens are now a major tourist attraction for visitors to Kildare.

Henry Greer's success was followed by tragedy; his two sons were killed in action in the First World War while serving with the Irish Guards. Lieutenant Frank Greer was killed on 10 February 1917; his brother, Lieutenant Colonel Eric Greer, was killed on 11 August 1917. The officers were each awarded the Military Cross. Henry Greer was knighted in 1925 and also became a senator in the new Irish Free State in that year. He died at Curragh Grange in 1934, aged seventy-nine.

Captain Darby Rodgers later owned Curragh Grange, and sold it to Joe McGrath Junior in 1958. Curragh Grange became the Sundai International College, known locally as the Japanese School.

DAN DONNELLY 1788-1820

A limestone obelisk erected in 1888 marks the site on the edge of the Curragh of Kildare known as Donnelly's Hollow. Dan Donnelly was born in Dublin in 1788, and was one of seventeen children. Over six feet tall, little else is known of him or his early life other than that his father was a carpenter and Dan followed him in the trade.
He was discovered by Captain Kelly, an eccentric racehorse trainer from Maddenstown, on the edge of the Curragh. Kelly lodged him at his brother's house in Calverstown, near Kilcullen, and trained him in the art of bare-knuckled boxing. Dan Donnelly was to fight twice at the Curragh, the first time in 1814 against Tom Hall from the Isle of Wight, before 20,000 spectators and for the prize money of 100 sovereigns. He beat Hall easily. His second fight before a great crowd took place in December 1815 against George Cooper. The fight lasted eleven rounds and ended with Donnelly knocking Cooper senseless to the ground. As Dan left the arena, his supporters made moulds of his footsteps. These steps can still be seen today – they are 'The steps to strength and fame'.

In July 1818 he beat English champion Tom Oliver at Crawley Hurst near London, where £100,000 in wagers changed hands. Dan Donnelly was reputed to have been knighted Sir Dan Donnelly in a tavern after the fight by the Prince Regent, later King George IV. Sir Dan died penniless on 18 February 1820 aged thirty-two.

Dan's body was interred in the Bully's Acre, Kilmainham, but was lifted by body snatchers or 'Sack 'Em Ups', and sold to a Dublin surgeon, who removed the right arm from the body for the purpose of examining the muscle structure. For many years Dan's arm was on display in the Hide-Out public house in Kilcullen, but was removed following the sale of the premises.

An obelisk that was erected on the Curragh in 1888 to mark the site where Dan Donnelly fought Tom Hall and George Cooper.

ELLEN DEASE

Ellen Dease (1820-1889) was born on 4 May 1820 at Firmount House, Clane. Her father was a surgeon in the British navy. Ellen was the youngest of five children and was educated at her home and later in Dublin. Her aunt took her to France and Italy where she studied languages and became fluent in several languages. Ellen was also a talented musician. Her biographer Kathleen McGovern described her as 'A very well educated cultured lady of the Victorian ideal'. After returning home Ellen entered Loreto Abbey in Rathfarnham. Health problems caused her to leave the abbey for a time. She returned and was professed there in 1847. On her profession, Ellen took the name Sister Mary Teresa Dease.

The bishop of Toronto, Bishop Power, corresponded with the Mother Superior at Rathfarnham in 1845. He asked her for volunteer sisters who would go to Toronto and set up a Loreto convent there. Because the Great Famine was raging in Ireland, the Mother Superior was not in a position to respond until 1847. She decided to send out five sisters, led by Mother Ignatia Hutchinson. Ellen, now Sister Mary Teresa, was one of the five who were chosen – she had taken final vows only two days earlier. The five left Dublin for Canada on 5 August 1847. On their way through the city they were met with a large crowd of mourners. It was the funeral of the 'Liberator' Daniel O'Connell and the city was thronged with people.

They traveled first to Liverpool, where they stayed for a few days before boarding a sailing ship, which took them to New York. From New York they took a river steamer, which brought them up the Hudson to Albany. Another journey by train took them to Lake Ontario. Their arduous journey finally ended after they crossed the lake in a boat to reach their final destination, Toronto. It was 16 September and the journey had taken almost six weeks.

They waited on the quayside with their luggage, but nobody was there to meet them. After some time they hired a coach, which eventually took them into the poorer area of Toronto, where they found the bishop's house. The news from the bishop was not good. He was reluctant to invite them in and informed them that Toronto was in the grip of a plague. It was called emigrant fever or ship fever, which was a form of typhus. Irish emigrants who had fled the famine had carried it over on the so-called coffin-ships, and the bishop informed them that two of the priests in the house had the fever. It was decided to send them to the house of a friend to await the opening of the convent.

The first Loreto convent was opened in Duke Street, Toronto, and was to be the first of many. Three of the nuns were constantly unwell. One of them, Sister Bonaventure Phelan, suffered from tuberculosis and died on 11 April 1849. In July of that year a newspaper carried a report on the first annual examinations taken in the school. Among the subjects mentioned were music, needlework, drawing, painting, and flower-arranging. The following year saw more health problems and Sister Gertrude Flemming died on Christmas Day 1850. She had for some time been suffering from gangrene. On

Firmount House, the birthplace of Ellen Dease.

9 March 1851 the superior died, leaving only two remaining sisters, one of whom was Sister Mary Teresa Dease. They had no choice but to close the school temporarily.

Bishop Charbonnell, who corresponded with the Mother Superior at home, had replaced Bishop Power. He wished to appoint Sister Dease as superior in the Toronto institute. The school soon reopened with the appointment of Sister Dease and some new postulants who had been sent from Ireland. Following her appointment, the convent entered a new period of expansion. Sister Dease remained in Canada for thirteen years before returning to Ireland for a visit. On 23 February 1860 she arrived in Ireland and was said to be looking better than when she sailed for Canada thirteen years previously. By this time she had established four houses in Canada West. She returned to Canada in June of that year.

During her thirty years in Canada she only made two visits to Ireland. On one of these she visited Fermoy, where her sister was Reverend Mother in the Loreto convent. In 1877 the Loreto order in Canada was given papal approval. Sister Mary Teresa Dease died in 1889, and was laid to rest in the convent grounds overlooking Niagara Falls.

The Flatsbury Stone in the ruins of St James' church, Johnstown.

FLATSBURY STONE

In the ruined medieval church of St John the Baptist, in the village of Johnstown, is preserved a tombstone that once marked the grave of James Flatsbury. Carved on the stone are the family arms and those of his wife Elenor Wogan of Rathcoffey. He died about 1436 and so the monument could date from sometime after that. The date 1289, cut in the centre of the cross, is probably inaccurate.

The Flatsburys were among the largest landowners in Co. Kildare between the thirteenth and seventeenth centuries. These lands included Johnstown and Palmerstown, later owned by the Bourkes, Earls of Mayo. James Flatsbury was described as a 'worthy gentleman and diligent antiquarie' who in 1503 compiled the famous *Red Book of Kildare* for Geroit More FitzGerald, the eighth Earl of Kildare. The latter, known as 'the Great Earl', was married to Alison, daughter of Roland Eustace, Lord Portlester. The O'Mores of Leix killed the earl while he was watering his horse in the River Griese at Kilkea in September 1513. *The Red Book of Kildare* is now preserved in the library of Trinity College Dublin.

In 1517 James Flatsbury wrote *The Chronicles of Ireland from 1184-1370* at the request of Geroit Oge FitzGerald, the ninth Earl of Kildare. The ninth earl later drew down upon himself the hatred of Cardinal Wolsey and nearly lost his head. The earl's son, 'Silken Thomas', tenth Earl of Kildare, was not so lucky: he was hanged, drawn and quartered at Tyburn in February 1537.

In 1641, six Flatsbury brothers took the side of the confederate Catholics and were all outlawed and had their estates confiscated. The Flatsbury name then disappeared entirely from Irish history, and by the beginning of the nineteenth century no trace of the family was to be found in Kildare.

FR JOHN SULLIVAN S.J.

John Sullivan (1861-1933) was born at 41 Eccles Street, Dublin, on 8 May 1861. He was the youngest child of a mixed marriage. His Protestant father, Sir Edward Sullivan, was called to the Bar in 1848 and enjoyed a brilliant legal career. He went on to become Lord Chancellor of Ireland in 1883. His mother, Elizabeth Josephine Baily, a Catholic, was the eldest daughter of Robert Baily, a wealthy property owner who lived at Passage West in Co. Cork. In accordance with the agreement made between his parents, John was raised a Protestant and was baptized in St George's Church, George's Place, which is near Eccles Street. In 1863 the family moved to 32 Fitzwilliam Place, and in 1873, John Sullivan entered Portora Royal School, Enniskillen, where his brothers had all been educated.

John was a very able and diligent student, and a large number of his awards and medals are preserved in the museum at Clongowes Wood College. John retained a deep affection for his old school throughout his life, especially for the headmaster, Dr William Steele. In 1879 John entered Trinity College, Dublin, and took his degree in 1883, receiving a gold medal in Classics.

Sir Edward Sullivan died suddenly in 1885. Not long after this, John left Ireland to commence his legal studies at Lincoln's Inn, and was called to the English Bar in 1888. Little is known of his career as a barrister. He seems never to have appeared in English courts but there is evidence that he appeared in Irish courts before Judge William O'Brien at Cork, as well as at Limerick, Killarney, Carlow, and Naas.

John Sullivan was received into the Catholic Church on 21 December 1896 by Fr Michael Gavin S.J. at Farm Street, the renowned Jesuit monastery in London. His life as a Catholic was marked by extraordinary fervor from the very beginning. After his conversion to Catholicism he became a frequent visitor to the hospice for the dying at Harold's Cross, Dublin. There he talked to and consoled the patients. He also became involved with the night refuge at Brickfield Lane, which was run by the Sisters of Mercy. From the time of his conversion to Catholicism he felt drawn to the priesthood, and in 1900, after only a few years in the church, he entered the Jesuit Novitiate at Tullabeg, Tullamore, Co. Offaly.

Fr John Sullivan SJ (1861–1933).

On 8 September 1902, John Sullivan took his first vows in the Jesuit chapel at Tullalbeg. On the completion of his novitiate he was sent for two years of philosophical studies to St Mary Hall, Stoneyhurst, England. Afterwards he studied theology in Milltown Park, Dublin, in preparation for his ordination. John Sullivan was ordained by Archbishop Walsh in the chapel at Milltown Park on Sunday 28 July 1907. Soon afterwards he was appointed to the teaching staff at Clongowes Wood College, where he was to spend most of the rest of his life. His work in Clongowes consisted of teaching, being Spiritual Father to the boys and working in the People's Church.

Despite the rigors of the ascetic lifestyle for which he was renowned in the locality of Clane, he enjoyed good health until the beginning of February 1933. The first sign of trouble was a swelling in his arm that confined him to bed for a fortnight. On the morning of Friday 17 February he suffered violent pains and was removed immediately to St Vincent's Nursing Home, Dublin. He was operated on that afternoon, but with little success. He died on Sunday 19 February 1933. Fr John Sullivan was buried in the community graveyard at Clongowes Wood. In 1960 his remains were exhumed and brought to Gardiner Street, Dublin.

FR JAMES HAROLD

Fr James Harold (1745-1830) was born in Dublin and educated in France, and was ordained there in 1780. On his return to Ireland he served as curate in a number of parishes. He was appointed parish priest of Saggart in 1794 by Dr Troy, Archbishop of Dublin. During the 1798 rebellion, Fr Harold preached two sermons, in which he urged his flock 'to shun all disorder and discord'. At the same time, he courageously rebuked the yeomanry and militia for their cruelty.

Shortly after this event, Fr Harold was arrested while saying Mass. It is said that he had harbored a wounded rebel called Felix O'Rourke from Blackchurch near Rathcoole, Co. Dublin, and was betrayed by a parishioner. Fr Harold was imprisoned for several months on a ship's tender, the *Lively*, in Dublin Bay, probably to thwart attempts to rescue him. His lawyers got a writ of *habeas corpus*, but the ship's captain refused to accept it. Eventually, the fifty-five year old priest was tried in Green Street courthouse and sentenced to ten years. Transported in the convict ship Minerva from Cobh, he arrived in Sydney in January 1800, after a ten-month voyage, and was detained in the convict colony of Botany Bay.

Later Fr Harold was sent to Norfolk Island, described as a terrible place reserved for the worst criminals. This penal settlement was closed in 1807, and the now aging and infirm priest was sent to Tasmania for a short period and then released. He arrived home to his beloved Dublin in 1815, his health broken. Dr Troy appointed him to the parish of Clontarf, and with the help of the Carmelites he built the first Roman Catholic church in Fairview in 1819.

Fr Harold never forgot his fellow convicts and he spoke out frequently about the cruelties of the penal colony and as a result of his representations to the authorities, a Cistercian, Fr Flynn was appointed chaplain to the penal colony. Finally, in 1815, Fr Harold was appointed parish priest of Kilcullen, Co. Kildare, and died on 15 August 1830, a venerable eighty-five years old. He is buried in Goldenbridge Cemetery, Inchicore. His wooden cross and pewter chalice are in the possession of Mrs Mary McNally of Rathcoole, Co. Dublin.

The only memorial to Fr Harold is Harold's Cross, Dublin, which was named after his family, who lived in the district.

FR MOORE'S WELL

One of many holy wells in Kildare, Fr Moore's Well is renowned locally for the many cures obtained by people visiting it. Fr Moore was born in 1779 at Rathbride near Milltown. He lived with his mother in a thatched cottage, now demolished, not far from where the well is located. Fr Moore had a remarkable gift for effecting cures

Fr Moore's Well, which was enclosed and renovated in 1952.

Fr Moore's Well, which is named after Fr John Moore.

of various ailments, and before his death he blessed the well in order that those performing the Stations of the Cross at the well might still be cured after his death.

He was ordained in Maynooth College in 1803, and was curate in the parish of Allen. He died at the age of forty-seven on 12 March 1826, and is buried at the west end of the ruined church in Allen. The people of Rathbride and the surrounding district renovated and enclosed the well in 1952.

FR THOMAS MURPHY

Close to the parish church of Our Lady and St David on the Sallins Road, Naas, is Fr Murphy Place, a small development of houses for senior citizens in the community. The year 2006 marks the centenary of the birth of Fr Thomas Murphy (1906-1945), in whose memory these houses are named. Thomas Joseph Murphy was born on 25 March 1906, the seventh child in a family of seven boys and four girls. His parents were Thomas and Mary Murphy, who lived at Fair Green, Kilcullen Road, where Swan's of the Green is now located. Thomas Murphy's father was a carpenter in Naas Workhouse, now Naas General Hospital; his family was a model of self-sufficiency in those days, having cows and a dairy, poultry, pigs and a large vegetable garden.

Like his brothers, Thomas attended the Christian Brothers School in the Moat (now the Moat theatre). Many of his brothers became tradesmen in the building trade. Thomas himself was apprenticed to the bar and grocery trade in the then well-established business of Staples-Dowlings, (later Mulveys) on Main Street, Naas.

Thomas Murphy received his secondary education at Mungret College, Limerick, and his clerical training at the Columban Seminary at Dalgan Park, Galway, and was ordained to the priesthood on 21 December 1935.

After his ordination Fr Tom traveled home to Naas to celebrate his first Mass on 22 December 1935. The *Leinster Leader* reported the occasion:

> Fr Murphy celebrated his first Mass at 9 o'clock in the Church of Our Lady and St David Naas on Sunday last He was assisted by Very Rev. M. Norris P.P. and Rev. L. Bennett, CC. The congregation as if cognizant of a very solemn and important occasion participated in the Holy Sacrifice with unusual fervor and devotion and intoned the responses to the young priest's prayers at the close of the Mass with great clarity and earnestness.

In May 1936 Fr Tom, along with five other newly-ordained Columban priests, was appointed to the new mission in Burma. Before he set out on the long journey, he spent a few months at home with his family, visiting relations and friends throughout the country and assisting the priests of Naas Parish. The *Leinster Leader* of 3 October 1936 carries a report of a special meeting of Naas Urban District Council to make a presentation to Fr Tom, prior to his leaving for the missions in Burma. For this special meeting the Chairman, Mr James Dowling, vacated the chair to allow Fr Norris P.P. to be chairman for the night. The people of Naas parish made a presentation of £107 to Fr Murphy. There was also a presentation by St Joseph's Young Priests' Society and the Caragh Samaritan Committee. Fr J. Bennett made the presentation, which consisted of a portable altar, including various sacred utensils for the celebration of Mass, and a set of priest's vestments. Fr Tom in his thanksgiving speech said: 'The money has been given as a personal gift, that has been stressed to me, but I assure you it will not be used outside the needs of the Maynooth Mission. It is a very fine offering and the people have shown great generosity in giving it, and I thank them very sincerely, as well as the many other nameless ones who have been generous to me not only now, but during all the years of my studies'.

In October 1936 Fr Murphy and five others left from Tilbury Dock, London, to embark on the long journey that would bring them to Burma. On first arriving in Burma, new languages had to be learned and Fr Tom went to Nanhlaing, north of Bhamo, to learn Shan. Most of Fr Tom's missionary work was among the Shan people in Nanhlaing, but also involved long and difficult journeys into the surrounding hill and jungle villages.

Although the Second World War was raging in the Far East it did not impact on the Columban missionaries until the arrival of Japanese soldiers in Bhamo in 1942. This interrupted the mission work, and all the Columban priests in Burma ultimately found themselves sharing accommodation with three hundred lepers in St John's leper asylum living there under the care of about one hundred nuns.

Fr Tom Murphy (1906-1945).

On the morning of 6 March 1945 there was intense shelling close to the leper asylum, where a British unit had dug in. As Fr Murphy was saying Mass with his companions, a stray shell exploded right above them. Several priests were injured, but none so severely as Fr Tom, who suffered severe foot and stomach injuries. In spite of valiant efforts to get medical assistance, Fr Tom died before he could reach a field hospital.

Little did the people of Naas know that when they said goodbye to Fr Murphy as he left for Burma missions in May 1936, it would be his last time among them.

LA TOUCHE OF HARRISTOWN

Harristown House was the home of the La Touche family for over 150 years. The family, who were Huguenots, fled religious persecution in France and settled in Holland. David Digues La Touche came to Ireland as a Williamite soldier towards the end of the seventeenth century and fought at the Battle of the Boyne. La Touche had three sons. The eldest, David, settled at Marlay Park, Co. Dublin, and was the first governor of the Bank of Ireland. The second son, Peter, inherited his father's estate at Bellevue, Delgany, Co. Wicklow. The third son, John, purchased Harristown Estate in 1768. Harristown was an old Eustace estate with a charter from Charles II, creating it a free borough with a corporation consisting of a sovereign and twelve burgesses that had the privilege of returning two members to parliament

Harristown House, the seat of the La Touches.

John La Touche enclosed the estate and built a boundary wall. This wall changed the line of the road from Naas to Dunlavin, which originally ran through Harristown Estate, across what is one of the oldest surviving bridges on the Liffey. To complete the road around the estate, he built a new bridge over the Liffey at Carnalway, which has a date stone with the year 1788 written on it.

John la Touche was known as 'the Master of Harristown' and was a member of the Church of Ireland. The family had helped to re-build St Patrick's Church on the edge of the estate to the design of the architect James Franklin Fuller. Fuller also designed the present Harristown house after a disastrous fire in 1891. The original late-Georgian house was three stories over a basement built according to the design of Whitmore Davis.

The 'Master' caused something of a sensation in Kildare after coming under the influence of a Victorian evangelist, Rev. C.H. Spurgeon. He became a member of the Baptist community and in 1882 he had the Baptist church and manse built at Brannockstown, with a school and teachers' residence. John La Touche had three children: Emily, Rose, and Percy. Rose La Touche's romance with the Victorian writer John Ruskin is well documented and recounted by Rev Robert Dunlop in his 1988 book *Waters Under The Bridge*. He was pastor of the Baptist church in Brannockstown from 1964 until his retirement in 2004. The 'Master' died in 1904 and was succeeded in the estate by his son Percy. Percy La Touche was the last of the family to live at Harristown, and he is remembered in Kildare for his passion for hunting, and for being a typical country gentleman of Kildare. He died in 1921. Harristown House and Estate were purchased by Major Beaumont in 1946, and is presently owned by Hubert Beaumont.

KILKEA CASTLE RENT TABLE

Formerly at Maynooth Castle, the rent table was carved in 1533 for the Earl of Kildare. The FitzGeralds later brought it to Kilkea Castle. It was the cause of much controversy in recent years when it was removed from the castle grounds.

KILKEA CASTLE

Kilkea Castle was a medieval stronghold of the FitzGeralds, Earls of Kildare. Sir Walter de Riddlesford built a moat and bailey here in 1181. A granddaughter of his married Maurice FitzGerald, third Baron Offaly, and so the Manor of Kilkea came into the possession of the FitzGeralds and was to remain in the family for the next 700 years.

The castle is particularly associated with Gerald, the eleventh Earl of Kildare, known as the 'Wizard Earl,' who became the male representative of the Geraldines when only twelve years of age, after his half-brother 'Silken Thomas', the tenth Earl, was executed at Tyburn in 1537.

1 Carbury Castle, a Tudor-Jacobean manor house.

2 Cloncurry church.

3 Courtown House rebuilt in 1815 by John Aylmer – the earlier house was sacked and burned during the 1798 Rebellion.

4 Cross shaft, Old Kilcullen.

5 Donadea Castle, principal seat of the Aylmers.

6 Kilteel Castle, an important tower house of the Pale.

Above: 7 Maynooth College, established in 1795.

Left: 8 Portlester effigy, New Abbey, Kilcullen.

9 Taghadoe Round Tower.

10 The Wonderful Barn, built in 1743.

11 Celbridge Charter School, built in 1732 to the design of Thomas Burgh. It is now a hotel.

12 The grave of Richard Soutwell Bourke, sixth Earl of Mayo, Viceroy of India.

Above: 13 Kerdiffstown House.

Right: 14 Great Connell standing stone.

15 Killashee House, built in 1863. The inscription over the entrance reads, 'Unless the Lord buildeth this house, the labour is vain.' It is now a hotel.

Right: 16 Newbridge College, by the
River Liffey, was established in 1852.

Below: 17 Oakley Park built in 1724 for
Arthur Price, Vicar of Celbridge.

18 The old RIC Barracks, Straffan (note the gun loops for defence).

19 Oldtown House, Naas, home of the De Burgh family for 300 years.

20 Palmerstown House, home of Richard Southwell Bourke sixth Earl of Mayo.

21 The Pyramid Tomb, Naas.

22 Rathcoffey House, built on the site of a Wogan castle for Archibald Hamilton Rowan.

23 A round tower and Romanesque doorway, Castledermot.

24 Straffan House, built for the Bartons, is now the world-renowned K Club.

25 The Tickell Fountain, Eadestown.

26 Tipper Cross, dated 1616.

27 Belan Temple.

28 Kilkea Castle, home of the Fitzgerald family for 700 years.

29 Rope marks and a benchmark on Devonshire Bridge over the Grand Canal near Sallins.

30 St Wolstans, the thirteenth-century priory of Augustinian canons.

31 The Baptist church in Brannocktown, built in 1882 for John La Touche of Harristown.

32 Barretstown Castle, built in 1853 for Rev. Erasmus Dixon Borrowes.

33 Carnalway House, built for Thomas Tickell.

34 Curragh Grange, designed by Richard Orpen and built in 1904.

Left: 35 Detail on the Conolly Obelisk, which dates from 1740.

Below: 36 Digby Bridge and Canal Lock, built in 1794.

37 Donnelly's Hollow.

38 Entrance to the ice house, Castlemartin.

39 The tower of Allen, built in 1859 by Sir Gerald Aylmer of Donadea Castle.

The FitzGerald rent table at Kilkea Castle before its removal.

The 'Wizard Earl' was sent to the Continent to be educated and following his return to Kildare his interest in alchemy caused much talk among his neighbors, and he was said to possess magical powers. The Earl died in 1585 and is believed to return to the castle every seventh year, mounted on a silver-shod white charger. In 1634 the castle was leased to the Jesuit order by the fourteenth Earl's widow, and remained in their possession until 1646. That year the order entertained Archbishop Rinuccini Papal Nuncio to the Confederation of Kilkenny, at Kilkea Castle.

In the early eighteenth century, the nineteenth Earl of Kildare decided to make Carton at Maynooth the family seat. Kilkea Castle was then leased to a succession of tenants. One of these tenants was Thomas Reynolds, a Dublin silk merchant, who was a 'friend', of Lord Edward FitzGerald, the Kildare hero of 1798 through whom Reynolds had become a United Irishman, only to turn informer. His role as informer did not prevent the castle, which had been recently done up in fine style, being sacked by the military during the rebellion. After a fire in 1849 the third Duke of Leinster resumed possession of the castle and restored it as a dower house for the family.

Kilkea Castle was the home of Lord Walter FitzGerald, son of the fourth Duke of Leinster. He was a founder member of the Kildare Archaeological Society in 1891, and the greatest antiquarian Kildare ever had. He was editor of *Journals of the Association for the Preservation of the Memorials of the Dead in Ireland* from 1904 until his death in 1923. When the FitzGeralds sold Carton house in 1949 Kilkea Castle became the seat of the eighth Duke of Leinster. It was eventually sold by the FitzGeralds in the 1960s, and is now a hotel and country golf club.

Above: The Evil Eye at Kilkea Castle.

Left: Kilkea Castle, the home of the FitzGeralds for over 700 years.

KILLEEN CORMAC

The ancient burial site of Killeen Cormac is situated in the townland of Colbinstown. This old cemetery is in a picturesque valley through which the River Griese flows, separating the counties of Kildare and Wicklow at Killeen Cormac. The site is remarkable for two reasons: firstly it is an ancient pagan cemetery adapted to Christian use, and secondly it is the only place in the county of Kildare where Ogham-inscribed stones are known to have existed. King Cormac is said to have been a King of Munster, and a great dispute arose regarding the place of his sepulture, as two powerful clans each wished to bury the body in their own territory. At last, to prevent bloodshed, it was agreed that the bier containing the body 'should be placed on a wagon, yoked to a team of seven unbroken bullocks, which were allowed to follow their own instincts in conveying the body to the place of burial'.

A pillar stone at Killeen Cormac.

The Kilgowen Standing Stone.

After traveling a long distance, the team of bullocks approached the Doon of Ballynure from the Timolin direction. Here the bullocks were overcome with exhaustion due to thirst, but – on pawing the ground – they found a spring of water, which gushed forth and can be seen to this day by the roadside, to the southwest of Ballynure Church. (The water from this spring is said to cure colds). After satisfying their thirst, the team proceeded a little further, and upon descending from the high ground they came to what is now called 'Bullock Hill'. Here, a hound that lay on its master's bier leapt forward and landed on the Killeen, leaving the impression of one of its paws on the standing stone. The team of bullocks proceeded, crossed the River Griese, and on reaching the Killeen, refused to go further. It was decided to bury King Cormac at this spot.

Around 1830, Killeen Cormac was enclosed by a stone wall and trees were planted on the mound by John Bonham, a local landlord who lived nearby at Ballintaggart House. Within the enclosures, lying on the terraces, were some inscribed pillar-stones with Ogham inscription. One of these is bilingual, with a Latin epigraph and Ogham inscription. This stone is now preserved in the National Museum. A companion pillar-stone with the face of Christ incised on it can be seen inside the entrance gate of Killeen Cormac.

A hunting party at Kilmorony House.

KILMORONY HOUSE

Travelers on the Athy to Carlow road will be aware of the gaunt ruins of a house that stands on an eminence above the River Barrow. This house was once the home of the Weldon family. The Weldons came to Ireland around 1600 and acquired considerable estates in Co. Laois and Co. Kildare. It is through Walter Weldon of St John's Bower in Athy County Kildare, that the direct line of the Weldon family in Ireland can be traced. In 1613 he was the MP for Athy, and in 1624 High Sheriff of Co. Kildare.

Over the next three centuries members of the Weldon family played an active and prominent role in the life of Kildare county. The family papers in the National Archives show the family's social contacts through correspondence with such prominent people as Winston Churchill and Douglas Hyde. The Weldons were essentially a military family, and many members served the British Empire in India, Africa and the Far East.

Captain George Anthony Weldon of the Royal Dublin Fusiliers was killed at Glencoe in October 1899 during the Boer War. Another member of the family, Major Arthur Stewart Weldon, served in South Africa and the First World War, and was killed in action in March 1917. His brother-in-law Colonel Croshaw died of wounds received in September 1917 during the First World War. The old British Legion Hall in Naas (now the Naas Scout Den) was dedicated to their memory.

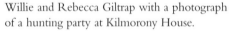

Willie and Rebecca Giltrap with a photograph of a hunting party at Kilmorony House.

Capt. George Anthony Weldon, who died in the Boer War.

The last of the male line of the Weldons to live at Kilmorony was Sir Anthony Arthur Weldon, who became the sixth Baronet of Kilmorony on the death of his father in 1900. Sir Anthony died in 1917 as a result of shell shock while fighting in France during the First World War.

The main entrance to Kilmorony Estate was on the Athy Carlow road, and is now obscured by road widening. The entrance avenue to the house was unique in that it crossed over the Barrow Navigation Canal and the River Barrow. The canal bridge is of cut stone, and the Barrow Bridge of iron construction. Part of the iron bridge had collapsed into the river and in recent years was dismantled and removed from the river.

Referred to as 'Sportland' on the 1783 Taylor map of Kildare, Kilmorony was a fine Georgian house built sometime after 1752 (it does not appear on the Noble & Keenan Map of 1752). The main block was of two stories over a basement of five bays with a balustrade roof parapet and a lower two-storey wing of four bays. The house was dismantled in the late 1930s. The coach house of Kilmorony has survived and is now a private dwelling.

Above: Kilmorony House, the seat of the Weldons.

Right: The Weldon coat of arms.

Kilteel Castle.

KILTEEL CASTLE

Kilteel Castle, a gateway with flanking tower, is situated near the site of an early monastery. The monastery and castle were part of a preceptory of the Knights Hospitallers of St John of Jerusalem. Maurice FitzGerald, second Baron Offaly, who died in 1257, founded the monastery here. It was dedicated to St John the Baptist.

Kilteel was an important border fortress of the English Pale. The monastery was suppressed in 1541 by Henry VIII and, with the castle, was granted to John Alan. At its dissolution, John Alan was also granted the Priory of St Wolstan's near Celbridge.

Carton House

Lord Edward FitzGerald (1763-1798).

LORD EDWARD FITZGERALD

Lord Edward FitzGerald (1763-1798) was born at Carton House, Co. Kildare, on 15 October 1763, the twelfth child of Emily and James FitzGerald, first Duke of Leinster. After the death of his father in 1773, his mother took the family to France, where they lived until 1779. Edward began his military career when he joined the Sussex Militia. He then served with the 96th Infantry in Ireland, and in 1780 he was appointed to a Lieutenancy in the 26th Regiment of Foot, then stationed in the south of Ireland. He was later posted to America where he saw active service and was severely wounded at Eutaw Springs in 1781.

Edward returned to Ireland, where he became a Member of Parliament for Athy in 1783. By 1788 he had rejoined the army, and made an adventurous journey to Canada through unexplored territory. He subsequently returned to Ireland and in 1790 became a Member of Parliament for Kildare, but resigned his seat in 1793 after an extraordinary outburst against the government.

He visited France, adopted revolutionary ideas, and renounced his title. While in France he married a French girl named Pamela, reputed to be the daughter of the Duke of Orleans. Pamela later became a courier for the United Irishmen in Kildare. On his return to Ireland he was given Leinster Lodge in Kildare town as a wedding gift, and it was here that he lived with his young bride. In 1796 he joined the United Irishmen and his home became a meeting place for the members.

With his military training Lord Edward was well suited to his position as military commander of the United Irishmen. His political beliefs were influenced by French revolutionary ideas. He supported the doctrines of enlightened thinkers such as Paine and Rousseau and believed in liberty, equality, fraternity, and the Rights of Man.

Following the arrests of the Leinster Directory of the United Irishmen in March 1798, Lord Edward went into hiding. The government offered £1,000 reward for his arrest and on 19 May Lord Edward was discovered at a house in Thomas Street, Dublin. After a struggle he was shot and wounded in the right shoulder by Major Charles Sirr. A militia officer was also killed in the struggle. Lord Edward was brought to Newgate jail where he died of his wounds on 4 June 1798. He was buried in St Werburgh's church, Dublin. The capture of Lord Edward, one of the few United Irish leaders with military experience, was a major blow to the organization. The compelling story of the life of Lord Edward is recounted in Stella Tillyard's *Citizen Lord*.

LORD WALTER FITZGERALD

Undoubtedly the greatest antiquarian Kildare ever had, Lord Walter FitzGerald (1858–1923), was the son of the fourth Duke of Leinster. He was educated at Eton College and the Royal Military College, Sandhurst, served in the 4th Battalion 60th Rifles, and saw service in India. He retired from the army in 1888, having attained the rank of captain, and was a member of the Carlow Militia from 1888 to 1898. Following his retirement from military life he devoted his time and energy to scouring his beloved Kildare as well as the south and west of Ireland in search of antiquities. He researched the history of the landed families of Co. Kildare, including his own, as well as tombstone inscriptions, place names, archaeology, and military history.

He was a founder member of the Kildare Archaeological Society in 1891, and attended its inaugural meeting at Palmerstown House (seat of the Earl of Mayo). He was its Honorary Secretary from 1894 until his death in 1923. Lord Walter contributed many articles to its journal under his own name, and under the pseudonym Omurethi. He was editor of the *Journals of the Association for the Preservation of the Memorials of the Dead in Ireland* from 1904, supplying almost all the illustrations and four-fifths of the

Lord Walter FitzGerald's grave in the ruined church at Kilkea Castle.

content. Lord Walter was a member of the Royal Society of Antiquaries of Ireland, and vice-president of the Royal Irish Academy. Lord Walter died at Kilkea Castle, the ancestral home of the FitzGeralds, on 1 July 1923; he was buried in the church ruins beside his sisters in the grounds of his beloved castle.

The Lord Walter FitzGerald Prize for Research is awarded biannually by Kildare Archaeology Society. The title of the prize (initiated in 2001) commemorates the fact that Lord Walter was a founder member of the society and contributed a vast number of learned articles to the journal. It was decided to award the 2001 and 2002 prizes to persons who had achieved lifetimes of research. The 2001 medal was awarded, posthumously, to Lena Boylan in recognition for her contribution to historical research in Kildare. The award for 2002 went to Lt. Col. Con Costello in recognition of his services to the written history of County Kildare over many years. Chris Lawlor won the first public competition in 2003 for his essay on Dunlavin entitled 'Sir Richard Bulkeley and the Foundation of Dunlavin Village'. The 2005 prize was awarded to Hugh Crawford for his essay 'The Kildare Lock Hospital'.

MARY LEADBEATER OF BALLITORE

Mary Leadbeater (1758-1826) was born at Ballitore into a Quaker family. She was the daughter of Richard Shackleton – a schoolteacher – and his second wife Elizabeth Carleton. The village of Ballitore in south Kildare was founded by the Quakers (Society of Friends) in 1707. Abraham Shackleton, Mary's grandfather, originally came from Yorkshire. He founded a boarding school at Ballitore, and became its first master when it opened on 1 March 1726. Richard, Mary's father, was a close friend of Edmund Burke and was educated with him at the Ballitore School. Mary too was well-educated, and was interested in reading from an early age. She read

French and English philosophers. When old enough, she was taken to London by her father, where she was introduced to Edmund Burke, Sir Joshua Reynolds and Maria Edgeworth, the author of *Castle Rackrent*.

In 1791, Mary married William Leadbeater who was a farmer, house builder and owner of a livery service. Mary became postmistress of Ballitore, and was a prolific writer. She is best remembered for *The Annals of Ballitore*, an account of events in the village from the years 1766 to1824 including the 1798 Rebellion. *The Annals* were published in 1862 as *The Leadbeater Papers*.

Left: A plaque on Mary Leadbeater's house in Ballitore.

Below: Mary Leadbeater's house, Ballitore.

From her diaries and letters it is possible to explore the events of the 1798 insurrection from a woman's perspective. Her writing gives us an eyewitness account of daily life at Ballitore, and also of the events surrounding the Rebellion. She recorded the violent scenes that were part of the daily life of the villagers in 1778. In Mary's later years she was always looking for ways to help the poor. She was in life and death a perfect embodiment of Quaker values: humble, unselfish and always a firm opponent of violence. Mary Shackleton Leadbeater died in Ballitore on 27 June 1826.

MAUDLINS CEMETERY

Maudlins Cemetery on the Dublin Road, Naas, was enclosed in 1772 by a wall and an imposing arched entrance of Wicklow granite. The inscription to the left and right of the entrance gate read, 'Lord Mayo to the inhabitants of Naas bequeathed a lasting habitation not made with hands'.

Many of the landed families from the Naas locality are buried here, including the Aylmers and Hendricks of Kerdiffstown; the De Burghs of Oldtown; the De Robecks of Gowran Grange; the Moores of Killashee; the Earls of Mayo of Palmerstown, and the Earls of Clonmel of Bishopscourt.

The entrance to Maudlins cemetery.

At the north end of the cemetery are the graves of General Walter Weldon and of his daughter Alice Frances Croshaw. His son Major Arthur Stewart Weldon was killed in action 25 March 1917 during the First World War. His daughter Alice was the widow of Colonel Oswald Mosley Croshaw D.S.O., who died of wounds received in action on 26 September 1917. The British Legion Hall in Naas was dedicated to their memory. The hall is now the Naas Scout Den.

The distinguished cartographer Alexander Taylor includes the cemetery on his fine 1783 map of Kildare.

MILLICENT HOUSE

Originally owned by the Keating family, Millicent House and Demesne were purchased by Richard Griffith in 1782. Griffith had made his fortune while working for the East India Company in Bengal. He was a member of the Irish Parliament from 1783 to 1790, and a director of the then newly-formed Grand Canal Company. Richard Griffith was High Sheriff of Kildare in 1788, and a captain of the Clane Yeomanry at the start of the insurrection in Clane and Prosperous on the night of 23 May 1798.

Richard Griffith's son, also named Richard, was to become one of Ireland's most renowned civil and mining engineers. He was born in 1784 and went to school in Portarlington. Later, while attending school in Rathangan, his school was attacked by the rebels during the Rebellion of 1798.

Noting that the rebels had placed green boughs in their caps, Richard thought it wise to do the same. When the rebels withdrew after the attack, a troop of dragoons arrived. The young student, still wearing his bough, found himself suspected of being a young rebel by the troops, who were on the point of summarily executing him. Luckily a local magistrate recognized their victim as 'young Griffith of Millicent'.

Millicent House, the home of Sir Richard Griffith.

Sir Richard Griffith (1784-1878).

From the 1830s onwards Griffith was involved in many major civil and engineering projects in Ireland. In 1828 he was appointed Commissioner for the General Survey and Valuation of Rateable Property in Ireland. This monumental work was given the title 'Griffith Valuation'. For his public service he was created a Baronet in 1858. Sir Richard lived at 2 Fitzwilliam Place, Dublin, from 1824 until his death in 1878 at the age of ninety-four. His house at Fitzwilliam Place is now the Hungarian Embassy.

Thomas Cooke Trench purchased Millicent House and Demesne in the nineteenth century. He built, at great cost to himself, the church of St Michael and All Angels on the edge of the demesne. This architectural gem, designed by James Franklin Fuller, replaced the old abbey church in Clane that had fallen into disrepair. Cooke Trench had been deeply affected by the disestablishment of the Church of Ireland, and he devoted the rest of his life to, as he put it, 'setting up again the pillars that had fallen down'.

MOONE HIGH CROSS

The best-known symbol of early Christianity in Ireland is the high cross. The development of high crosses bearing scriptural scenes had probably begun in Ireland by the second half of the eighth century. One of the earliest and certainly the most unusual of these high crosses is the cross of Moone.

This tall, slender granite cross, standing seventeen feet six inches high, was one of the first of its kind in Ireland to introduce scenes from the bible. The high and tapering base of the cross shows scenes from the Old and New Testaments. On the west face of the base are Adam and Eve, the 'Sacrifice of Isaac', and 'Daniel in the Lion's Den'. The north face shows, in descending order, 'The Three Children in the Fiery Furnace', 'The Flight into Egypt', and 'The Miracle of the Loaves and Fishes'. On the east face of the base we see a panel showing the twelve apostles and the Crucifixion. This last image was incorporated into the opening sequence of the renowned documentary series *Radharc* on RTE television.

Often referred to as St Columcille's Cross, the Moone monument stands on the site of a sixth-century monastery. Parts of the cross were found buried on the site in 1835, and this is probably the reason for its fine state of preservation. The cross was pieced together and erected in 1850, and the shaft was later discovered and added to it in 1893 by the Kildare Archaeological Society as one of its first projects after the society was founded in 1891.

In 1995 the high cross was restored by the Office of Public Works and relocated for preservation in the church ruins. On a visit the Clondalkin Historical Society, hosted by members of the Naas Local History Group, Mr Brendan Cullen (an authority on high crosses) noted that, when referring to their guide books, visitors to the cross should be aware that the orientation of the cross has been reversed with the recent relocation.

The Moone high cross, c.1851.

The Moone high cross before restoration and relocation.

MOORE ABBEY BAPTISMAL FONT

Preserved at Moore Abbey, Monasterevin is the most decorative late medieval baptismal font in Kildare. The font is carved from sandstone and is mounted on a reconstructed octagonal pedestal and base. The bowl of the font is tulip-shaped, and has eight panels with rounded arches set on pillars. Angels are carved in low relief in the panels and each holds an emblem of the faith:

Panel One: an angel holding a chalice.

Panel Two: an angel holding a cross.

Panel Three: an angel wearing a maniple.

Panel Four: an angel holding the sword of the spirit.

Panel Five: an angel holding a crosier.

Panel Six: an angel holding a thurible and incense.

Panel Seven: an angel holding an anchor.

Panel Eight: an angel holding a key and an orb with a cross on top.

Moore Abbey occupies the site of a sixth-century monastery founded by Saint Evin, from whom the town takes its name. At the time of the Reformation, Moore Abbey was acquired by Sir Adam Loftus, first Viscount Ely. In 1699 Jane Loftus, daughter of the third Viscount Ely, married Charles Lord Moore, and Moore Abbey therefore came into the possession of the Earls of Drogheda. Henry Moore, first Earl of Drogheda, held considerable estates in Dublin and had streets named for the family, including Drogheda Street, Moore Street, Henry Street, and North Earl Street.

The Earls of Drogheda continued to live in Moore Abbey up to the early years of the twentieth century. The house stood empty during the Troubles but did not suffer any destruction. Moore Abbey was later leased by Count John Mc Cormack, the renowned Irish tenor. He resided there with his family until 1938. The Sisters of Charity of Jesus and Mary purchased Moore Abbey in 1940, but they did not take up residence until after the end of the Second World War. Moore Abbey is now run as a residential facility for the intellectually disabled.

Above: The Moore Abbey baptismal font (detail).

Left: The Moore Abbey baptismal font..

NAAS BARRACKS

Built in 1813 as an infantry barracks to accommodate eighteen officers and three hundred men, Naas barracks was the home of many British regiments up until Irish Independence in 1922. Over the years it housed the Kildare Militia, the 6th Garrison Battalion, the Forfar Militia, and the 42nd Highlanders – otherwise known as the Black Watch, they came to Naas barracks in 1814. During the Crimean War, the barracks saw considerable military activity, with troops being mobilized for the Mediterranean area. In 1867 the 89th Regiment was sent from Aldershot to the barracks to assist in quelling the Fenian rising led by the Young Irelander William Smith O' Brien.

The Royal Dublin Fusiliers, formally the 66th Brigade, arrived in Naas barracks in 1881. The barracks was to be their depot for the next forty years. During the First World War many young Kildare men joined up at Naas barracks to fight on the battlefields of Europe and beyond, some never to return. During the War of Independence the barrack square was halved with a barbed wire fence in order to allow the Black and Tans to occupy one section. The last detachment of the Royal Dublin Fusiliers marched out of the barracks on 7 February 1922. They were destined for Bordon, in Hampshire, where they were disbanded on 31 July of that year. The barracks was handed over to Irish Free State forces, headed by Col. Comdt. Moylan, Brigadier Thomas Lawlor, and Captain John Joyce. There was no ceremony to mark the occasion. The flagpole had been cut down and removed, so that the tricolour could not be hoisted until the new garrison had located and erected a flagpole at the main gate.

Lt. Col. Fintan Mullowney.

The closing-down ceremony of John Devoy Barracks in 1998.

The Irish Free State army occupied the barracks until 1928, when it was closed down and handed over to the Office of Public Works. Up to the Second World War, some of the buildings in the barracks housed small industries, including a slipper factory, a sausage factory, and a printing works. In 1931 about half of the barracks was leased to Naas Cotton Mills. The County Kildare Vocational Education Committee also took over part of the barracks for their Technical School and offices. Naas Town Council took over the married quarters of the barracks in 1934, for local authority housing which they named St Patrick's Terrace

The Barracks was reopened in October 1956 as an apprentice school to train technicians for the army and naval service. The first commanding officer of the school was Lt Col. Jock McDonald. Always referred to as ' Naas Barracks' it was renamed Devoy Barracks in 1956 in honour of the Fenian leader John Devoy. The Apprentice School was under the command of Lt Col. Fintan Mullowney, a native of Naas, from 1984 to 1992.

Devoy barracks closed in September 1998, a sad occasion for the people of Naas. The barracks had been a part of the history of the town for nearly 200 years. After the closing ceremony, commanding officer Lt Col. Des Donagh presented Thomas O'Connor's painting of John Devoy (which had hung in the Officers' Mess in Devoy Barracks since 1956) to Naas Town Council. This painting now hangs in the Council Chamber of Naas Town Hall.

In 2002 the barracks was demolished, except for the archway. The Osprey Hotel now occupies part of the site. Also on the site is Aras Chill Dara, the new headquarters of Kildare County Council and Naas Town Council, completed in 2006.

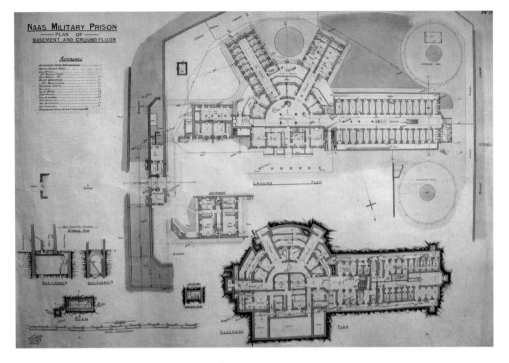

The 1886 plan of Naas Jail.

NAAS JAIL

Naas Town Hall was originally built as a jail in 1786, and figured prominently during the 1798 rebellion in the town. By 1820 it was considered unsuitable, and plans were drawn up for a new prison. The new prison, located to the south of the canal harbour, was completed in 1833 at a cost of £14,000.

A close look at a set of coloured drawings titled 'Naas Military Prison', gives an idea of the size and engineering complexity of the building. The drawings are dated 6 September 1886 and signed by Richard Stevens, temporary draughtsman, Royal Engineers. The first drawing shows the north elevation, and a plan of the prison. The plan gives details of graveled surfaces, flagged surfaces, underground drains, fresh-water pipes and hydrants, rain-water pipes, and gas lamps. The gas supply to the prison came from the gasworks on the canal. The gasworks commenced supplying Naas town in March 1865.

A second drawing shows the layout of the ground floor and basement. Located in the basement were the kitchen, storerooms, servant's rooms, windlass room, and workshop. Coal was stored in three bunkers in the basement to fire the furnaces and boilers. The laundry was also located in the basement. It had washing troughs, steam tubs, drying horses, and a cast iron cistern to store water to run the laundry. There was one padded cell, and seven solitary confinement cells in the basement. A lift in the basement serviced the ground, first and second floors of the prison.

Railings from the exercise yard of Naas Jail on Fair Green.

A surviving wall of Naas Jail.

A six thousand gallon water tank on the roof of the entrance block provided water to the prison. The water was pumped by a windlass from a well at the west end of the prison. The main prison block contained ninety cells and a further seventy-eight cells in the two wings. Six-inch steam pipes heated the cells, with ring main gas lighting throughout. The staff chapel was located on the ground floor, and the main prison chapel on the first floor, with the chapel gallery on the second floor. The infirmary was opposite the main jail block. On the ground floor were two wards; the surgery and kitchen. On the first floor were four wards with water closets and bathroom.

There were two exercise yards in the jail, each sixty feet in diameter, surrounded by six feet high steel railings. These railings were removed from the jail in the early years of the last century, and were erected along the edge of the fair green where Euro Spar supermarket now stands. The railings prevented livestock from wandering out on to the main road on fair days – the era of the motorcar had arrived!

Details of life in the prison are sketchy. However, an account book from the 1830s from the jail includes an entry recording that the barber was paid five shillings for shaving the heads of prisoners with fever. Other entries show that the hangman was paid £5 during the summer assizes. Local tradition holds that the hangings were carried out over the main entrance gate. Lists of prisoners at Naas jail for the years 1837-38 survive. These lists show that prisoners aged between sixteen and forty-two received sentences of transportation for life for assault, highway robbery, stealing cattle and sheep, and seven years for rape.

In 1861 by-laws were drawn up for the jail; staff was to include a governor, wardens, matrons, chaplains and a schoolmaster. Records were to be kept of punishments, and the retention of juveniles. Rising time was 6a.m., with lockup at 5.30p.m. The diet was stirabout, oaten meal, milk, gruel, soup and brown bread. The jail closed in the early 1890s, having been in operation for just sixty years. For the next sixty years the jail was used for many purposes, including housing for the people of Naas. The families lived in the old staff quarters, the infirmary, and the Governor's residence. Children born there had the unusual distinction of having been born in Naas jail.

In 1954 the cut stone from the main cellblock was used for the building of the new mortuary chapel in the Church of Our Lady and St David in Naas. The end came for the jail in the 1960s, when it was finally demolished to make way for St Martin's housing estate. A small section of the boundary wall is the only evidence remaining that indicates that a building of this size and structure ever existed in Naas.

NEW ABBEY EFFIGY

We find the double effigy of Roland Eustace and his wife Margaret D'Artois in New Abbey cemetery, Kilcullen. This effigy was originally part of an altar tomb inside the abbey church. The side panels of the Portlester tomb were built into the dwarf walls of the chapel. The carving on the panels represents various religious figures: St Francis, St Bridget, St Catherine, St Michael, the Virgin and Child, and symbols of the Passion and Crucifixion. One panel bears the Portlester arms, quartering those of Margaret D'Artois.

The effigy is now badly weathered as a result of lying prostrate, exposed to the weather, for many centuries. In April 2001 the effigy was relocated to its present upright position in a Gothic limestone surround by Kildare County Council.

Roland Eustace founded and endowed New Abbey for the Franciscans of Strict Observance. *The Annals of the Four Masters* recorded its foundation thus; 'The age of Christ 1486 the Monastery of Kilcullen for the Friars Minor de

The New Abbey effigy before relocation.   The New Abbey effigy in its new location.

Observantio was commenced on the banks of the Liffey, by Roland, son of Sir Edward Eustace of Castlemartin'. He was a generous benefactor of the church and had the Portlester chapel built in 1455, at the east end of St Audoen's Church, High Street, Dublin.

Roland Eustace was born around 1430, was knighted in 1459, and in 1462 was created Baron Portlester by Edward IV. He died in December of 1496 and was buried within New Abbey. Also buried in New Abbey were his daughter Alison, Countess Kildare, who died in 1495, and his nephew Viscount Baltinglass, who died in 1549.

New Abbey was suppressed by King Henry VIII in 1539, after only fifty-three years in existence, and within a few years was in ruins. In 1582 the abbey was forfeited, and let to the poet Edmund Spenser, who is said to have written part of his epic poem *The Faerie Queen* during his time living at New Abbey.

The tower of the friary fell in 1764. In May of 1784 a fire destroyed the chapel and a nearby mill. The chapel was rebuilt in 1837 with material from the old abbey and was described as 'standing within the cemetery'. This chapel continued to be used until a new parish church was built in Kilcullen. The new parish church of St Brigid and the Sacred Heart was built to the design of J.J. McCarthy R.H.A. and was dedicated in September 1872. Cardinal Paul Cullen officiated at the dedication ceremony.

Oakley Park, built in 1724 for Arthur Price, Vicar of Celbridge.

OAKLEY PARK.

Formerly known as Celbridge House, Oakley Park was built by Arthur Price in 1724, when he was vicar of Celbridge. The house is attributed to Thomas Burgh MP, Engineer and Surveyor-General for Ireland, whose descendants still live at Oldtown, Naas.

Arthur Price was educated at Trinity College, Dublin, and in later years became its Vice-Chancellor. In 1730 he was made Bishop of Ferns and in 1734 became Bishop of Meath. While Bishop of Meath he started to build the beautiful Ardbraccan House at Navan as a residence for the Bishop of Meath, although he continued to live at Oakley Park.

During the building of Ardbraccan House, Dr Arthur Price was made Archbishop of Cashel. It is recorded in Ware's *Antiquities* that 'it had been much to be wished that he never quitted Meath and then the house at Ardbraccan would have been finished and the noble and venerable cathedral on the rock of Cashel would have escaped his destructive hand'. By an Act of Council he 'removed' the cathedral from the Rock of Cashel into the town, uniting it with St John's Parish. He left the cathedral on the rock roofless, 'By which means that noble and venerable pile has gone to ruin'.

At Oakley Park, Dr Price's steward was Richard Guinness. One of his duties was to supervise brewing for workers on the estate. Guinness had acquired the reputation of

The hopper head of a rainwater pipe that is dated 1724, in Oakley Park.

being able to 'Make a brew of a very palatable nature'. Richard's son Arthur was born in 1725, and was named after Arthur Price who was his godfather. In 1759 Arthur Guinness bought a brewery at St James' Gate, Dublin, and started what is now the famous Guinness brewery.

In 1787 George Napier and his wife, Lady Sarah Napier, took up residence at Oakley Park. Two of Lady Sarah's sisters married into the wealthiest families in the county: Louisa married Thomas Conolly of Castletown, and Emily married James FitzGerald, nineteenth Earl of Kildare and first Duke of Leinster. Lady Emily was mother of the 1798 leader Lord Edward FitzGerald.

Colonel Napier sold Oakley Park in 1804, and for the next century the Munsell family owned the house. The Guiney family purchased Oakley in 1935 and later sold it to the Christian Brothers. The Christian Brothers intended opening an Industrial school there, but this plan did not come to fruition. In the early 1950s Oakley Park and lands were acquired by the St John of God Brothers, and are now part of the St Raphael complex, a residential institution for the disabled.

OLD KILCULLEN

St Patrick is said to have founded a bishopric at Old Kilcullen, over which he placed Bishop MacTail. There was an early monastery, on the site of which the incomplete eleventh-century round tower, now only eleven metres high, and traces of a Romanesque nave-and-chancel church survive. Portions of three stone crosses also survive, the granite shaft of the west cross having panels with fine carvings. The round tower and church were damaged in the fighting at Old Kilcullen during the 1798 rebellion. By the early years of the nineteenth century the church had fallen into ruin. St John's Church of Ireland at the Yellow Bog was built to replace this church, on land owned by the Borrows from the nearby Gilltown Estate.

The Old Kilcullen effigy, now in St John's Church of Ireland church, Ballymore Eustace, was originally in the church on Old Kilcullen hill, probably on an altar tomb. By 1781 the effigy had been moved outside, and is shown in an engraving of 1782 (see photograph), leaning against the wall at the south-west corner of the church. The effigy was damaged during the fighting at Old Kilcullen in 1798, and was said to have been used later as a paving slab under a pump.

Around 1850, Sir Erasmus Dixon Borrowes took the effigy to his residence at Barretstown Castle just north of Ballymore Eustace for safe-keeping. On the sale of the castle by the Borrowes family in 1919, the effigy was moved to its present location in St John's Church of Ireland church, Ballymore Eustace.

The Old Kilcullen Church and Round Tower in the eighteenth century.

An effigy from Old Kilcullen, now in St John's Church, Ballymore Eustace.

The round tower and cross shaft at Old Kilcullen.

PALMERSTOWN HOUSE

Lord Mayo's Beautiful Mansion in Ruins

At 9.30 on Monday night, Palmerstown, the Irish residence of Senator the Earl of Mayo and the Countess of Mayo, was entered by armed men who set the massive building on fire, destroying it and its contents.

Lord and Lady Mayo had finished dinner, and there were in the house at the time, two male and six female servants. Two young fellows knocked at the front door, which was opened by the butler. They demanded money, and he shut the door speedily without answering them. Some minutes later a knock came to the servants entrance, and the hall boy inquiring who was there, was answered, ' An orderly officer of the Irish Republican Army.'

He opened the door and three men entered, armed with revolvers. They left and returned in a few moments with petrol tins. They were met by Lord Mayo who asked what they wanted. They said they had come to burn the house 'as a reprisal for the execution of six men at the Curragh.'

Palmerstown House, which was completed in July 1874.

Palmerstown House, which was rebuilt after having been burnt by the IRA in January 1923.

They proceeded through the house, and sprinkled the main hall, dining room and drawing room with petrol. They allowed the servants a quarter of an hour to remove their personal belongings. Lord Mayo asked if they would give him time to remove his best pictures and his plate and they consented. The plate and some valuable pictures were removed, also the contents of the study, kitchen, scullery and housekeeper's room. In all about half an hour was allowed. Then matches were set to the saturated rooms and in a few moments the place was a roaring mass of flame.

The raiders left, having stated they could not wait and wanted to get back to Dublin. Military from Naas and the military fire brigade from the Curragh arrived on the scene, but nothing could be done to save the fine mansion, which was completely gutted. The offices and servants' quarters adjoining were saved.

Leinster Leader, 3-2-1923

PAUL CULLEN

Cardinal Paul Cullen (1803-1878) was born at Prospect House near Ballitore, Co. Kildare, on 29 April 1803 and was educated at the Quaker School there. He studied for the priesthood at Carlow College, and the College of Propaganda, Rome, where he was ordained in 1824. He became rector of the Irish College in Rome in 1832. He was appointed as Archbishop of Armagh and Apostolic Delegate in 1850. As a representative for the Irish bishops, he sought to counteract British influence at the Vatican. On his advice, Pope Gregory XVI condemned the new Queen's Colleges, and urged the Irish bishops to establish a Catholic university.

In 1850 Cullen summoned and presided over the first National Synod held in Ireland since the twelfth century, in Thurles, Co. Tipperary. He was transferred to Dublin as archbishop in 1852, and used his influence to improve social conditions by constitutional means. He abhorred the Young Ireland and Fenian movements, but his petition to the Crown saved the Fenian leader Thomas F. Burke from hanging. The founding of the Catholic University in 1854, and the appointment of Cardinal Newman as its first rector, were largely due to his support. He was a strict disciplinarian and worked hard to improve the morale and education of his clergy.

Cardinal Paul Cullen (1803-1878), the first Irish cardinal.

Archbishop Cullen founded Clonliffe College, the Dublin diocesan seminary, in 1859. He was a frequent visitor to Rome, and took a leading part in the First Vatican Council. He is said to have drafted the dogma on Papal Infallibility. The archbishop became Ireland's first Cardinal in 1866, died in Dublin in 1878, and was interred at Clonliffe College.

There is a commemorative stained glass window to Cardinal Paul Cullen in Crookstown church, near his birthplace in Co. Kildare.

PUNCHESTOWN STANDING STONE

The most perfect of the many standing stones in County Kildare, the Punchestown standing stone, has a place in the folk tales of Fionn MacCumhall. One such tale tells of Fionn throwing the stone from the hill of Allen to Punchestown.

The first historic reference to the stone is that made by Giraldus Cambrensis, who writes of 'the Giant's Dance' at the great stone not far from the fortress of Naas. Giraldus was born in Pembroke, Wales. His knowledge of Ireland derives from two lengthy visits to the east and south of Ireland in 1183, and again from 1185 to 1186, when he accompanied Prince John.

This great, tapered monolith of Wicklow granite, seven metres high, fell in 1931. Before the stone was re-erected in 1934 a small cist grave was discovered at the site.

RICHARD SOUTHWELL BOURKE

In St John's Church, Johnstown, a Celtic cross marks the grave of Richard Southwell Bourke (1822–1872), Lord Naas, sixth Earl of Mayo, Knight of the Most Illustrious Order of St Patrick. He was a distinguished statesman and scholar. At the age of thirty, in 1852, he was appointed Chief Secretary for Ireland. Because of his relative youth, he was called 'the Boy Secretary.' The chief secretary was the principal executive of government in Ireland in the nineteenth century. During his first period as Chief Secretary at the Chief Secretary's lodge in the Phoenix Park, he added a glass conservatory to the house, originally built in 1776. This house is now the residence of the United States' ambassador to Ireland. Lord Naas was MP for County Kildare from 1847 to 1852, and Chief Secretary again from 1858 to 1859, and again from 1866 to 1868. On the death of his father, fifth Earl, in 1867 Richard Southwell Bourke succeeded to the title as sixth Earl of Mayo.

Queen Victoria appointed the Earl of Mayo as Viceroy of India in 1868. He was assassinated on 8 February 1872, while on a tour of inspection on the Andaman Islands. His remains were brought back to Ireland and received with great ceremony by the Lord Lieutenant. Tradition says his body was transported home from India in a barrel of rum, hence his nickname 'the Pickled Earl'.

The Mullaghmast Standing Stone.

The Punchestown Standing Stone.

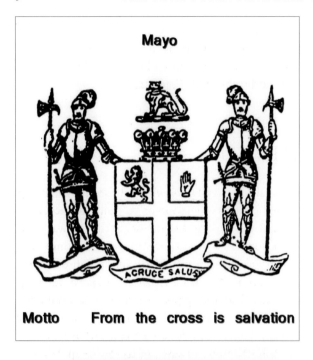

The Mayo coat of arms.

The grave of the sixth Earl of
Mayo, Viceroy of India.

The Mayo College in Ajmer, Rajasthan, India, is named in his honor. His family home, Palmerstown House at Johnstown, was re-built in the Queen Anne style by public subscription as a tribute to his memory. Palmerstown House was burnt during the troubles in 1923, and was later rebuilt by the Irish Free State.

ROBERTSTOWN CANAL HOTEL

In 1776, plans were submitted for a canal hotel at Lowtown, and the site eventually chosen was at Robertstown. William Semple won the contract to build the hotel and work commenced in 1799. Before long, it was reported to the board that he was using bad material for the masonry work 'and the walls are erected in a slovenly, imperfect and unsafe manner.' Two years later the hotel was still unfinished, and in February 1801 the board warned Semple that he had exceeded the time specified in his contract. He blamed the company's choice of site, which had a very poor foundation, for the delay because he had to remove one-and-a-half feet of crust, and use planks at the west end to form a solid base. Shortly after, William Semple was declared bankrupt. In May 1801 the canal board received a letter from John Semple, assignee of the bankrupt William, undertaking to complete the contract on receipt of £220 outstanding.

By the end of August 1801 John Semple reported that the hotel was almost ready: some work on the stairs remained to be completed, and the doors needed to be hung. The board authorized an additional expenditure of £600 to furnish it 'in a neat, plain and substantial manner.'

The canal company decided to run the hotel itself, and Allen McMillan, a former boatmaster, was appointed hotelkeeper with a weekly wage of one pound, two shillings and nine pence. The hotel was to be inspected every six months and 'if the House and Offices are in perfect repair, and the furniture no more damaged than ordinary that fair use will necessarily produce, the housekeeper shall receive over and above his weekly salary a gratuity of 26 guineas.'

The hotel was opened to boat passengers on 15 October 1801. The charges were one shilling and seven pence for state cabin passengers, and sixpence for common cabin passengers, with a charge of five shillings and five pence per night for any guest who stayed more than two nights. It was ordered that the passengers be respectfully acquainted, and that the chambermaids be prohibited from receiving gratuities of more than sixpence from each state cabin passenger, and three pence from each common cabin passenger. The charge for cleaning boots was not to exceed two pence, per pair, and for carrying luggage three pence per person.

A visitor to Ireland in 1803, Sir John Carr, who had traveled extensively in Europe, appears to have been most impressed by the amenities provided at Robertstown Hotel, which he described as 'The Noble Inn.' With the introduction of the faster flyboats on the canal, and an improved system of coach connections, the demand for accommodation in the canal hotels declined. By 1813 they were showing so great a loss that the company advertised them for letting as 'hotels or otherwise'.

The former Grand Canal Hotel, Robertstown.

'The Noble Inn' at Robertstown stayed in business. In 1815 Nicholas Whyte leased the hotel for £26 per annum, and in the 1820s a number of diocesan conferences were held in the hotel. Nicholas died in 1827, and his brother Robert took over the lease of the hotel.

Robert died in 1844, and his widow was left with four young children and continued to run the hotel with difficulty, until she surrendered the lease in 1849. Jasper Rodgers and his two sisters took the lease of the building in 1850, and it then ceased to be a hotel.

In 1869 the Royal Irish Constabulary leased the building as a barracks, at an annual rent of £42. Part of the building was converted into a residence for the district inspector of the RIC. The constabulary remained in occupation until 1905.

A Mrs Hughes took a lease of the district inspector's residence after it was vacated, and the rest of the building was used for occasional tenants. The government took over the building during 'Emergency', to house workers engaged in turf-cutting on the bog of Allen. It was used as a youth hostel in the early 1950s. Later it became a centre for the local branch of Muintir na Tíre. At the suggestion of local curate Fr P.J. Murphy, period banquets and annual canal 'Festas' were later held at Robertstown and the hotel regained, for a short period, some of its former glory. With the tragic death in 1975 of Fr Murphy, the driving force behind the venture, another chapter in the long history of 'The Noble Inn' came to an end.

St Patrick's Well, Barrettstown.

ST PATRICK'S WELL BARRETSTOWN

The grotto was originally built in 1938 by Pat Sweeney and Larry Donnelly. Restored by Clongorey Community Asssociation in February 2004, it was re-dedicated on St Patrick's Day in 2004.

ST WOLSTAN'S

The monastery of St Wolstan's, near Celbridge, was founded in 1202 by Richard, its first prior, and Adam de Heredford, for the Augustinian canons of St Victor. At the dissolution of the monasteries, St Wolstan's, with its rectories, mills, gardens, and one thousand acres of land, was granted to Sir John Alen, the Lord Chancellor. Austin Cooper, the eighteenth-century antiquary, made two trips to sketch the ruins of St Wolstan's, the first in May 1781, the second in May 1782.

The existing ruins are much the same as when Austin Cooper sketched them, but a tower shown in his sketch has totally disappeared. The tower shown in the photograph was repaired in the nineteenth century, and the figure of an angel in white marble was inserted over the south doorway.

The tower of the
thirteenth-century
priory of St Wolstan's.

St Wolstan's House was built by the Lord Chancellor's successor John Alen, who
is reputed to have been the architect of Jigginstown House, Naas, and said to have
been 'of great skill in architecture'. St Wolstan's was subsequently much altered in the
eighteenth and nineteenth century. The house was then in the possession of the Cane
family. Second Lieutenant Maurice Cane, Royal Field Artillery, was killed in action
on 4 August 1917 during the First World War.

The Sisters of the Holy Faith purchased St Wolstan's in 1955 and opened a boarding
school for girls. With the decline of applications, the school closed for boarders in
1984, and continued as a day school. St Wolstan's School moved to its new location
at Ballymakealy on the Celbridge to Clane road in 1999, and is now a community
school.

St Wolstan's House.

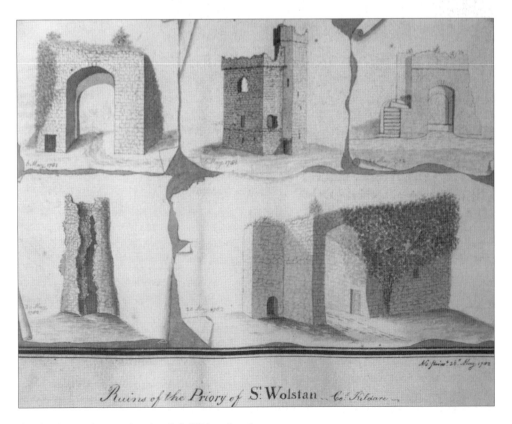

Ruins of the Priory of S. Wolstan Co. Kildare

Austin Cooper's 1782 sketch of St Wolstan's priory.

STRAFFAN HOUSE.

Richard de Clare, better known as Strongbow, bestowed the Straffan estate upon Maurice FitzGerald (ancestor of the Dukes of Leister) for his role in the Anglo-Norman invasion of 1169.

In the early years of the eighteenth century, Hugh Henry purchased the estate. He was a merchant banker who helped develop the early banking system in Dublin. Hugh Henry married Ann Leeson in 1717. She was a sister of Joseph Leeson, first Earl of Milltown, who had made a fortune from his breweries. The couple had two sons, Joseph and Hugh. Joseph, the eldest son, inherited Straffan estate. When Joseph came of age in 1748, he set out on the 'Grand Tour' of Europe, which was the custom of the time with people of wealth and privilege. His heir, John Joseph, married Lady Emily FitzGerald, a daughter of the second Duke of Leinster. John Joseph was one of the wealthiest men in the Ireland of his day, and he spent lavishly on Straffan House. One of his projects was the building of an underground passage from the house to the stables. In the end his extravagance forced him to sell Straffan House and estate and leave Ireland. He died in 1846, the estate having been purchased by the Bartons in 1831.

Straffan House, seen from the fountain, designed in 1853 by Val Dosne.

Hugh Barton (1766-1854) demolished the eighteenth-century house and commenced building a new mansion in 1832. An imposing house, it overlooks the River Liffey in a style like that of Italianate and French chateaux, with dormers in a mansard roof and elaborate decorated chimneys, dominated by a tall slender campanile with two tiers of open belvederes. James Howe laid out the formal parterre in 1863 to link the house to the river. The Victorian fountain is by Val Dosne Two suspension bridges, one by Courtney and Stephens, the other by Baily and Ross, lead to an island on the River Liffey. While building this new mansion the Barton family lived at Barberstown Castle. Hugh Barton also built the Church of Ireland church in the village of Straffan. Capt. F.B. Barton had the house reduced in size in 1937, and he sold the estate in 1949.

Hugh Barton was the grandson of Thomas Barton, who had established himself in the wine business in Bordeaux in 1725. During the 'Reign of Terror' in France many of the big merchants were imprisoned. Hugh Barton was apprehended, but with the assistance of his Bordeaux-born wife he escaped to Ireland. As he was forbidden to hold property in France, he arranged for his partner, Daniel Guestier, to take over and manage his business. This informal agreement lasted well into the nineteenth century, when it was formalized. The descendants of Barton and Guestier continue to manage their extensive vineyards in France.

John Ellis, who owned woolen mills in Yorkshire, purchased Straffan House in 1949. In the early 1960s Stephen O'Flaherty purchased the estate. He had imported Volkswagen cars into Ireland in the post-war years, and founded Motor Distributors. In the mid 1960s the house was owned by the film producer Kevin McClory, who produced the early James Bond movie *Thunderball* – he sold Straffan in 1978. The next owner was General Nader Jahanbani, the head of Iran's sports federation under the Shah. The General was executed by the Khomeini regime in 1979. Patrick Gallagher, the property developer, then purchased the estate. Alan Ferguson, a British mining millionaire, was the next person to purchase the estate. Dr Michael Smurfit purchased Straffan House and estate in 1988. He brought the world-renowned golfer Arnold Palmer to Straffan to create and design the K Club. This was selected as the venue for the 2006 Ryder Cup, the most prestigious competition in golf.

TAGHADOE ROUND TOWER

There are five round towers in Co. Kildare, located at Castledermot, Old Kilcullen, Kildare town, Oughterard, and Taghadoe, near Maynooth. The round tower at Taghadoe marks the site of a monastery founded by St Tua. Little is known about the history of the monastery. Near the tower is the ruin of an early nineteenth-century Church of Ireland church.

Taghadoe round tower, which is twenty metres high, like all of the round towers in Kildare, has lost its conical roof. Just below the top of the tower is a row of put-lock holes that penetrate the wall of the tower. These put-lock holes were used to attach scaffolding to each level during the construction of the tower.

The Taghadoe round tower and church ruins.

Maunsell Mausoleum and the Conolly Death House, Tea Lane Cemetery.

TEA LANE

Tea Lane in Celbridge is so called because workers from the nearby woollen mills on the River Liffey occupied the cottages along Church Lane. The workers loved their mug of tea and used to dispose of the tea-leaves in the lane leading up to St Mochua's Church and graveyard.

St Mochua founded St Mochua's church in the parish of Kildrought in the seventh century. He also founded a monastery with a round tower at Clondalkin. The church was used as a burial place for the Dongans of Castletown. Lord Walter Dongan, the last of the family to be buried there, was killed while fighting for King James at the Battle of the Boyne. Later the Conollys of Castletown House and the Munsells of Oakley Park were buried there.

The Conolly mausoleum, often referred to as the Conolly Death House, has a splendid monument by Thomas Carter to William Conolly (1662-1729) of Castletown House, who was Speaker of the Irish House of Commons. The effigies are of Conolly and his wife, Catherine Conyngham. The monument is vast and framed by four marble columns that support a massive pediment with the Conolly coat of arms. The figure of Conolly is semi-recumbent and his eyes are closed to indicate that he is dead. His wife Catherine gazes down, holding a prayer book in her left hand. Their monograms are worked into the railings in front of the monument. On a large marble plaque behind the monument, the inscription in Latin extols the virtues of Conolly. Translated and summarized it reads:

St Mochua's church, on Tea Lane, Celbridge.

He was a commissioner of revenue for twenty years. And Priory Councillor, twice elected Speaker, and ten times Lord Chief Justice. He was loyal, patriotic, firm, resolute, just, and wise. He made a modest though splendid use of the great riches he had honestly acquired. Gave instructions in his will that a building should be erected on the adjacent lands for the maintenance and education of the children of the poor and he endowed it forever with large revenues.

The building referred to on the inscription is the Charter School, erected by Conolly's widow Catherine in 1732. In recent times the effigies of Conolly and his wife were taken to Castletown House for preservation.

FAS restored the Maunsell Mausoleum and cemetery wall in 1995 at the behest of the late Lena Boylan, a noted local historian who did much to record the history of the area.

By the early nineteenth century St Mochua's Church had fallen into ruins. In 1813, with the support of Lady Louisa Conolly, a new Church of Ireland church was erected, according to the design of Sir Thomas Drew, inside the entrance gates to Castletown House. St Patrick's Catholic Church on the Main Street was built in 1857 to the design of J.J. McCarthy.

Teresa Brayton

TERESA BRAYTON

Teresa Brayton (1868-1943), poet and novelist, was born on 29 June 1868 in Kilbrook, Kilcock, near the famous 'Old Bog Road.' She was the daughter of Hugh and Elizabeth Boylan. Teresa attended Newtown National School and showed an interest in writing from an early age. At senior school she became a school monitor, a position usually given to good students who took some teaching duties and generally helped out in the classroom. She later worked in her old school, as an assistant teacher with her sister Elizabeth, for a short time.

Like many of her generation, Teresa left Ireland for America in September 1895. She settled in Boston first and later moved to New York. While there she met and later married Richard Brayton, a French Canadian who worked in the Municipal Revenue Department.

She became interested in politics while in America, and was an active supporter of the Irish Republican Brotherhood. Teresa is generally remembered as a folk poet of Irish America. As an activist, Teresa organized fundraisers and distributed political pamphlets. She returned to Ireland on a number of occasions, and was acquainted with many of the leaders of the 1916 Rising.

Her writing career began when she got some assignments for Irish-American newspapers. Teresa began to write poetry for such papers as *The Irish World*, New York, *The San Francisco Monitor* and many other publications. The pain of being away from her native country is one of the themes of her work. In her poem 'In Cappagh Hill' she describes how she dreamed of being back in Cappagh, but was shocked to awake to find she was on Broadway in New York. Teresa's great-grandfather had taken part

The grave of Teresa Brayton in Cloncurry churchyard.

in the Battle of Prosperous during the 1798 Rebellion, and she wrote poems for the centenary of the rebellion in 1898. Always aware of the political climate back home, and the struggles of the Land League and the National League, she campaigned for both. Teresa wrote nationalist poems on their behalf for local newspapers such as *The Nation* and the *Westmeath Independent*.

Her poem 'The Old Bog Road' became famous as the song of the Irish exile, and was set to music by Madeline King (later O'Farrelly), a native of Rochfordbridge, Co. Westmeath. Teresa has been compared to the Meath poet Francis Ledwidge. She strongly identified with her work, especially her poems of exile. The poem 'Rossa's Homecoming' is considered to be one of her most political. This poem is about the return of the body of Jeremiah O'Donovan Rossa, a Fenian.

In recognition of her efforts, Countess Markiewicz gave her a splinter from the flagpole that flew over the GPO during the 1916 Rising, 'as a tribute to your beautiful verses that are an inspiration to lovers of freedom and justice.'

Teresa returned permanently to Ireland in 1932, aged sixty-four. She settled first in Bray, Co. Wicklow, and later on the North Strand, Dublin, where she witnessed the bombing on 31 May 1941 during the Second World War. The last three years of her life were spent at Kilbrook, where she died on 19 August 1943. She was buried in the nearby Cloncurry cemetery. Enfield Muintir Na Tíre erected a Celtic cross over her grave, and President Eamon de Valera performed the unveiling ceremony on 18 October 1957. In his oration he spoke of the importance of Teresa Brayton as a revolutionary poet. Many of her memorabilia are displayed in the Teresa Brayton Memorial Library in Kilcock.

THE THIRTEENTH MILESTONE

The first turnpike road in Ireland was set up from Dublin to Kilcullen. in 1729 Turnpike roads were the equivalent of modern-day toll roads. Brian McCabe, a local historian from Johnstown, located the last surviving milestone on the Naas-Dublin road in 2002. The milestone was buried in undergrowth along the wall of the old Mayo Estate, just off the then north-bound dual carriageway. The granite stone is square, half a metre in height, and is inscribed on two of its faces. The east-facing side has the number 13 engraved above the letters DUB, while the north-facing side has the letters NAAS and the number 2 engraved underneath. The miles on the stone are Irish miles – 2240 yards (compared to the Statute mile of 1760 yards), and were measured from Dublin Castle.

Taylor and Skinner's maps of the roads of Ireland, from 1777, shows all the milestones on the old road, from just inside the Dublin boundary to Jigginstown House beyond Naas. On the map, the thirteenth milestone is clearly shown just outside Palmerstown Estate, then the seat of John Bourke, Lord Naas, and later Earl of Mayo.

Local historian Brian Mc Cabe examines the thirteenth milestone.

The thirteenth milestone on Taylor and Skinner's 1778 map of the roads of Ireland.

The old toll-road system was created on major arterial routes to ensure that the burden of road maintenance was not borne by the inhabitants living in the areas through which they passed. The Irish toll-road system failed to generate sufficient income to fund proper maintenance, and local inhabitants resented the double-taxation of tolls and county taxes. The coming of the railways in the nineteenth century hastened the demise of the toll roads. Following a commission of inquiry in 1855–56, the turnpike trust was disbanded.

A date stone from 1745 on a bridge over the River Blackwater, known as 'the Bishop's Chair'.

THE BISHOP'S CHAIR

There is a bridge over the River Blackwater in the townland of Hortland, in North Kildare, that is known as 'the Bishop's chair'. A date stone on the bridge bears the inscription, 'This bridge was built by Josiah Hort, Lord Archbishop of Tuam one of his Majesties most honorable privy councilors in ye year 1745'. In the same year, he had a windmill built at Hortland, and the date stone read: 'This mill was erected by his grace Josh Hort, Archbishop of Tuam 1748'. The mill was demolished, but its outline is still evident where it stood.

Josiah Hort was born near Bath in England in 1673, and was educated at Clare College, Cambridge. In 1709 he became chaplain to the Marquess of Wharton, Lord Lieutenant of Ireland. He was appointed Dean of Cloyne in 1718, Dean of Ardagh in 1720, Bishop of Ferns in 1721, Bishop of Kilmore in 1727, and was appointed Archbishop of Tuam in 1742. He married Elizabeth Fitzmaurice, a niece of the first Earl of Kerry in 1725. The archbishop's second son, Sir John Hort, first Baronet of Hortland, married Margaret, daughter of Sir FitzGerald Aylmer of Donadea

Hortland House, designed by the German architect Richard Castle, was built for Archbishop Hort in 1748. The house had two storeys, with five bays. There was a Venetian window with Doric pilasters above a tripartite doorway, with a fanlight and baseless pediment. By the early years of the twentieth century, Hortland House had fallen into disrepair, and was subsequently demolished. The gate lodge survives.

Archbishop Hort died in 1751 and was buried in the churchyard of St George, Dublin. Sir Arthur Fenton Hort, sixth Baronet, was the last member of the family to hold the Hortland estates in Co. Kildare.

The Dunboyne chandelier in St Patrick's College, Maynooth.

The Dunboyne coat of arms.

THE DUNBOYNE CHANDELIER

Preserved in St Patrick's College, Maynooth, is the Dunboyne chandelier. This chandelier was presented in 1770 by Reverend John Butler, Catholic Bishop of Cork. For many years it hung in the church of St Finbar in south Cork, and subsequently in the parish church in Bantry, Co. Cork.

Pierce Butler, eleventh Baron of Dunboyne, died unmarried in 1785, and was succeeded in the Dunboyne estates by his uncle, Bishop Butler, who became twelfth Baron Dunboyne. The bishop, by then seventy years of age, caused a sensation by resigning and converting to the Church of Ireland. He married his young cousin in what proved to be a vain attempt to provide an heir to the Dunboyne estates. He lived with his young wife between Dunboyne Castle, his town house in Leeson St, Dublin, and Gracefield House, which was his summer residence in Balbriggan, Co. Dublin. He was reconciled to the Catholic Church before his death on 7 May 1800. Having failed to produce an heir, he was succeeded by his cousin James Butler, thirteenth Baron of Dunboyne.

John Butler made a will – against the advice of the Catholic archbishop of Dublin – leaving his Meath estates, which included Dunboyne Castle, to Maynooth College. His sister Catherine, who had married William O'Brian Butler from Bansha, Co. Tipperary, disputed the will. A legal battle ensued, and as a result only part of the estate was granted to Maynooth College. The revenue from the settlement went towards funding the Dunboyne Establishment for Higher Ecclesiastical Studies at Maynooth. The other part of the estate, which included Dunboyne Castle, went to Catherine O'Brien Butler. Dunboyne Castle, an eighteenth-century house on the site of the ancestral Butler castle, became a convent of the Sisters of the Good Shepherd. The town house in Leeson Street became a convent of the Sisters of the Sacred Heart. Gracefield House, his summer residence, became a Loreto convent in 1857, but sadly it was demolished in recent years.

The inscription on the orb of the chandelier is in Latin amd translated it reads,

The pious and devout sodality for the visiting and relieving of the sick and poor established and approved under the patronage of the Immaculate Conception of the Blessed Virgin Mary by the most illustrious and Reverend John Butler Baron Dunboyne Bishop of Cork, in the year of Our Lord 1766, the third year of his Episcopate – dedicates presents and consecrates this chandelier as a token of its affection, in the year of the Lord 1770.

THE LEWIS BROTHERS OF NAAS

In 1915, when soldiers fought and bled to death in Flanders and the Dardanelles, three Lewis brothers from Back Lane in Naas served in three different units. Michael was serving with the Second Dublin Fusiliers in France, Patrick was serving with the First Dublin Fusiliers at Cape Helles in Gallipoli, and Thomas was a gunner with the Royal Field Artillery.

Michael, concerned about his brother Patrick, wrote to his sister Bridget on 19 April 1915:

> Dear Sister,
>
> I received your fond and most welcome letter, and was very sorry to hear Patsy was gone to the Dardanelles. I hope he will get through it safe. I hope he will write to you soon. I thought he was in the base, if he is along with the Coughlans he won't be lonesome, but that is where there is great danger.

Michael ends his letter to Bridget with a poem:

> When twilight fills
> The evening sun
> And pins it with a star
> Remember once you are a
> Sweet heart no matter where
> You are

On 25 April 1915, six days after he wrote this letter, Michael was killed in action as the Second Dublin Fusiliers tried to retake the village of St Julien, which had been lost to the Germans the previous day. The counter-attack failed and losses were dreadful: they were all highly-trained regular soldiers, and at that stage of the war they were irreplaceable. The Dublins lost 510 men of all ranks, who were either killed or wounded. Sgt. William Cooke from Kilcullen won a DCM here.

On the same day, Sunday 25 April, the First Dublins landed at Cape Helles Gallipoli, in the Dardanelles, between Greece and Turkey.

Before he went to the Dardanelles, Patrick Lewis wrote a letter to his mother from Victoria Barracks, Cork.

> My Dear Mother,
>
> Just a few lines, hoping to find you in good health as this leaves me at present. I am going in the next draft. I was for the doctor's inspection on Sunday after coming off the

Michael Lewis' name on the Menin Gate at Ypres, Belgium.

Thomas Lewis in 1940.

Nun's guard. I am going to the first battalion they are in England after coming home from India, I don't know whether they are going to France or where. I hear we are going to Egypt, about fifty of us with the first Battalion, We are going to England to join them Jim Mc Combs is here. I heard no account of Mike yet only from your letter. I was sorry to hear of Mr Haydon's death, I wish I had taken his advice about the army.

Tell William Stafford I was asking for him and Patrick Malone. Tell them I was asking for them, tell them I am going out with the first battalion that came home from India. They are in England, we are going in two or three days, it was along time threatening but it has come at last. It will cripple all the young fellows of the world. It is a pity to see them, fine young fellows going around here crippled. Paddy Hackett is in my room he is home from the front I think I have no more to say at present.

 Write soon don't delay a minute, in case I would not be here. I don't know the minute I might not be here.

No.4385 Pte. P. Lewis
B Company 3 R.D.F.
Victoria Barracks. Cork.

After horrific casualties on V Beach in the Dardanelles the remains of the First Dublins and First Munsters were formed into a composite battalion. Affectionately named 'the

No. 16708/E
(If replying, please
quote above No)

Army Form B 104-82

Infantry Record Office
25 MAY 1915
Island Bridge, Dublin.

Madam,

It is my painful duty to inform you that a report has this day been received from the War Office notifying the death of No 5348   Rank Pte.   Name Mchl. Lewis Regt 2:R DUBLIN FUS.   which occurred at the Front on the 25th day of April 1915   and I am to express to you the sympathy and regret of the Army Council at your loss. The cause of death was   Killed in Action.

Any application you may wish to make regarding the late Soldier's effects should be addressed to 'The Secretary War Office, Whitehall, London S.W.1 and marked on the outside 'Deceased Soldier's Effects'

I am,
Madam,
Your obedient Servant

Mrs K. Lewis.   Wm. Cooney Capt.
For O i/c Records No 11 District

The War Office notification of the death of Michael Lewis.

No 16708 E
(If replying, please
quote above No.)

Army Form B 104-82.

Infantry Record   Record Office,
Office
18 MAY 1915   Station.
Island Bridge
Dublin.
————————— 191

Madam,

It is my painful duty to inform you that a report has this day been received from the War Office notifying the death of No 4385   (Rank) Pte.   (Name) Patrick Lewis   (Regiment R. DUBLIN FUS.   which occurred while serving with Mediteranean Exped. Force on the 11th day of May 1915 and I am to express to you the sympathy and regret of the Army Council at your loss.   The cause of death was killed in action .

Any application you may wish to make regarding the late soldier's effects should be addressed to 'The Secretary, War Office, Whitehall, London S.W.' and marked on the outside 'Deceased Soldier's Effects'

I am,
Madam,
Your obedient Servant.

C. Chrimp Capt.
For O.i/c Records No. 11 District
Officer in charge of Records

Mrs K Lewis

The War Office notification of the death of Patrick Lewis.

Dubsters', with the strength of eight officers and four hundred men, the unit was ordered back to the front and engaged in savage fighting as the Turks tried to drive the invaders into the sea. Patrick Lewis was killed in action on 11 May 1915 at Cape Helles, Gallipoli, just two weeks after his brother Michael. The next day, the Dubsters were withdrawn for rest and refitting and resumed their battalion identities.

Patrick was buried with his fallen comrades in the war cemetery at V Beach, Cape Helles, in Gallipoli. Michael's body was not identified; his name is recorded on the Menin Gate in Belgium, along with so many others from the 'war to end all wars.' The last surviving brother, Thomas, was wounded on 27 July 1916. Originally missing, feared dead, he was later confirmed as wounded in action. He survived the war and lived in Naas until his death in the early 1970s.

Lance Corporal Peter Coughlin, Second Royal Dublin Fusiliers, mentioned in Michael's last letter, from Rathasker Road, Naas, was killed in action in France on 1 March 1917. Both Jim McCombs and Paddy Hackett, mentioned in Patrick's last letter, survived the war. A total of 567 Kildare men who had joined the British armed forces were never to return from the First World War.

THE WELLESLEY TOMB CHEST

In the south transept of Kildare Cathedral lies the tomb chest of Bishop Walter Wellesley, who was prior of Great Connell, near Newbridge. Great Connell, an Augustinian Abbey, was founded in 1202, and dedicated to Our Lady and St David. In the Middle Ages Great Connell was one of the most important Anglo-Irish monasteries, and the prior was a Lord Spiritual of Parliament.

Walter Wellesley was appointed prior of Great Connell around 1521, and became Bishop of Kildare in July 1529. Bishop Wellesley was interred at Great Connell Abbey in a tomb chest, which he had commissioned for himself prior to his death, in the autumn of 1539. Under the guidance of the Kildare Archaeological Society, the tomb chest was taken from Great Connell in 1971 to Kildare Cathedral for preservation. The funds to relocate the monument were provided by the seventh Duke of Wellington, a kinsman of prior Walter. Great Connell Abbey is now so decayed that scarcely any descriptive account can be given of the remaining ruins.

This monument in Kildare Cathedral is considered by scholars to be one of the finest surviving tomb chests of the sixteenth century in Ireland. The tomb chest consists of an effigy of Bishop Walter, mounted on side panels that are decorated with carvings of the Apostles, an Ecce Homo, a Crucifixion, and what is probably the only representation on a tomb chest of a Sheela-na-Gig in Ireland.

The marginal inscription reads, in translation

Here lies Brother Walter Wellesley former Bishop and commendatory Prior of this house on whose soul may God have mercy.

The tomb chest of prior Walter Wellesley in Kildare Cathedral.

Great Connell abbey, which was founded in 1202.

A Sheela-na-Gig on the underside of the Wellesley tomb chest.

Austin Cooper's 1782 sketch of Great Connell abbey.

The Tower of Allen,
c.1900.

THE TOWER OF ALLEN

The hill of Allen has always been associated with the Fianna and Fionn Mac Cumhaill. The great bog of Allen that almost surrounds the hill stretches west to the River Shannon. The hill was an ideal site for Sir Gerald George Aylmer, eighth Baronet of Donadea Castle, to build a tower that would have a commanding view over his property, and be a lasting memorial to his 'gallant tenantry'. The tower was begun in 1859 and finished in 1863.

The work was carried out during the summer months, as the location was too exposed for the masons to work during the winter months.

Known locally as 'Aylmers Folly' the tower is eighteen metres high and stands on the summit of Allen Hill, which is 206 metres above sea level. The limestone for the building of the tower was quarried near Edenderry, County Offaly, and brought to Robertstown by canal barge, and on to Allen hill by horse and cart. The granite copingstones came from the quarries at Ballyknocken, County Wicklow.

Steps in the Tower of Allen with the names of some of the construction workers.

The building material was brought to the hilltop on a four-wheel wagon. The wagon wheels were said to have been borrowed from two of the three cannon guns at Donadea Castle. Sir Gerald Aylmer had the name of each labourer who worked on the construction of the tower cut into one of the eighty-three steps of the tower as 'an everlasting memorial to them'. The two stonemasons who built the tower were Lawrence and William Gorry. Their names are inscribed on the landing stones at the top of the winding stairs. Carved on the copingstone on the inside top of the tower is the following inscription:

In thankful remembrance of God's mercies many and great. Built by Sir Gerald Aylmer, Baronet A.D. 1860.

There was also a glass dome, which has since disappeared, which was set over a circular viewing stand on top of the tower to protect the viewer from the inclement weather.

The visit of the Prince of Wales (afterwards King Edward VII) to the tower is recorded with the following inscription on the flagstones, between the iron railing and the base of the tower:

Sept. 16th A.D. 1861, H.R.H. The Prince of Wales ascended this tower.

The Tickell Fountain at Eadestown, erected in 1899.

TICKELL FOUNTAIN

Travellers on the Naas-Blessington road will be aware of the decorative drinking fountain at Eadestown. The Co. Kildare tenants of Commander Thomas Tickell R.N. erected this fountain to express their appreciation of his helping them to improve their living conditions. They also subscribed towards the erection of a memorial gateway to him at St Patrick's Churchyard, Carnalway.

Thomas Tickell's great-great-grandfather had come to Ireland in the early part of the eighteenth century as secretary to the Lord Lieutenant. He built Tickell house on his Glasnevin estate, now the home of the director of the botanic gardens. He married Clotilda, daughter and co-heiress of Sir Maurice Eustace of Harristown, Kilcullen in 1726, thus inheriting many of the townlands in that part of the county. Their grandson, Thomas Tickell, built Carnalway House overlooking the River Liffey, and the house is now part of Newberry Stud. He died in 1831 and is buried with his wife in St Patrick's Churchyard, Carnalway.

His son Edward purchased a large tract of land along the old Woolpack Road, which included the Steeplechase course of Punchestown, from the Duke of Leinster. Edward Tickell died unmarried in 1863, and was succeeded by his nephew – Commander Thomas Tickell R.N., in whose memory the fountain was erected. The Kildare estates of the Tickells encompassed 2240 acres in 1876.

Carnalway House, which was built for Thomas Tickell.

Thomas Tickell died in 1898 and was succeeded by his son Edward, a noted amateur rider, big-game hunter, and international swordsman and revolver shot who competed in the Olympic Games of 1912. Edward presented the 'Tickell Cup' to Punchestown racecourse, to be competed for by local riders.

There were negotiations to have the fountain erected at Poplar Square, Naas, but this plan did not materialize. The fountain, designed by J.J. O'Callaghan, was erected on the present site in 1899.

In the early years of the last century, the fountain was much appreciated by the farmers of West Wicklow because it allowed them to water their livestock on the way to the plains of Kildare.

TIPPER CROSS

Located in Tipper churchyard, near the ruins of a pre-Reformation church, stands a well-preserved cross. In his *Memorials of the Dead*, Vol. 5, Lord Walter FitzGerald states that it is the oldest monument in the churchyard. On the east face of the cross is a representation of the Crucifixion. Above the Crucifixion scene are the letters *INRI* (meaning 'Jesus of Nazareth, King of the Jews', in Latin). Below it are the letters *IHS* (the first three letters of the name Jesus in Greek). Further down the shaft is the date *1616*.

On the west face of the cross is an *IHS* across the arm; below, on the shaft, is a shield bearing the Delahyde coat of arms, and below it are the initials *J.D.* and *M.W.*, the last letter being on the side of the cross shaft. Underneath the initials is another shield bearing the Walsh coat of arms.

The east face of Tipper Cross, dating from 1616.

Tipper Cross, the west face.

Lord Walter was able to identify the initials J.D. and M.W. as being those of John Delahyde and his wife, Margery Walsh. John Delahyde died on 13 of January 1616, which is the year carved on this memorial cross.

WALTER HUSSEY BURGH

Walter Hussey Burgh (1742-1783) was born on 23 August 1742, at Donore House, Caragh. His father was Ignatius Hussey, and his mother was Elizabeth Burgh of Oldtown, Naas. Elizabeth was the daughter of Thomas De Burgh, who was MP for Naas and Surveyor General of Ireland. Walter Hussey entered Trinity College Dublin, distinguished himself in the classics, and graduated with a Bachelor of Arts degree. He married his cousin, Anne Burgh of Bert House, Athy. When he inherited half of the property of his maternal cousin Richard Burgh of Drumkeen, Co Limerick, in 1762, he adopted the additional name of Burgh. Walter Hussey Burgh was called to the Irish Bar in 1769 and in November of that same year he was elected member for Athy in the Irish House of Commons.

In 1776 he was chosen to represent Trinity College. He had published a letter in *Anthologia Hibernica*, in reference to his candidature to represent Dublin University. In the letter he stated the firmness and independence of his political views, and the high sense he entertained of the duties of a representative in parliament. He rose fast in the ranks of the legal profession and his success later elevated him to the high rank of Prime Sergeant, which at that time was one of the most important distinctions in Ireland.

After his election as MP for Athy he took an active interest in government affairs. Hussey Burgh was considered one of the best orators in the Commons. Wellesley claimed that Burgh was superior in style to Pitt, Fox and Burke. He was renowned for his response to the assertion that Ireland was at peace, 'Ireland is not at peace: it is smothered by war. England has shown her laws as dragons-teeth, and they have sprung up as armed men'. For this speech Hussey Burgh got a standing ovation in the House. He then announced that he had resigned the office he held under the crown, at which Henry Grattan exclaimed, 'The Gates of promotion are shut, but the gates of glory are opened to Hussey Burgh'.

He was a supporter of the Roman Catholic cause and said of the popery laws:

This cruel code is not founded, as some assert, in necessary policy, but religious persecution. Ireland is a subordinate country, and its great object is to guard against the oppressions of England. Our great object then should be to relax the unnecessary severity of the laws that separate society into two classes, oppressors and slaves. Internal discord has been the ruin of the ancient republics. Let us learn wisdom from experience and try what union may effect in the renovation of ours.

Hussey Burgh, along with Henry Grattan, advocated free trade. In 1779 he moved the resolution 'That it is not by temporary expedients but by free trade alone, that this nation is to be saved from impending ruin'. He was appointed Chief Baron of the exchequer following the procurement of a measure of independence by the Irish parliament in 1782.

His lifestyle was lavish, having houses both in town and country. Following his death it was revealed that he was not a wealthy man. He died at Armagh at the age of forty-one, leaving a wife and five children in poor financial circumstances. Following Hussey Burgh's death, Henry Grattan arranged a government pension for the family.

The ruins of Donore House, the birthplace of Walter Hussey Burgh.

The Wonderful Barn, built in 1743.

THE WONDERFUL BARN

The Wonderful Barn was built by the Conollys of Castletown House on their land near Leixlip. It was built in 1743 for the purpose of famine relief after the severe winters of the early 1740s. Major Hall's Barn at Rathfarnham, built at the same period, was probably modeled on the Wonderful Barn. The barn is one of the finest and most unusual follies in Ireland. Unlike many other follies of the period, which were largely ornamental, the Wonderful Barn had a very practical use.

The barn is conical in shape and has seven floors. Grain was hauled to the floors by windlasses through a trapdoor in the center of each floor. The grain was spread out for drying, and then sacked for storage. Ninety-four steps wind round the outside of the barn like a corkscrew to a height of seventy-three feet. The southwest face of the barn is weather-slated and the windows are triangular.

The barn is situated in one corner of a rectangular courtyard, with pigeon houses on two other corners. These pigeon houses were built to house pigeons bred for the table at Castletown House and are similar in structure, though smaller than the barn. The pigeons fed off the grain that was lost from the carts taking the grain to the barn. The original pigeon-nesting boxes are still in place.

This architectural gem is in need of urgent care and should be taken into public ownership. Over the entrance door a date stone reads:

1743 Executed by John Glin